# SEVEN
# CREATIONS
## AGRICULTURE TO GOD

GENE WUNDERLICH

# Contents

In the Beginning was the Dog
Settlement and Agriculture
Grasses and Other Plants
Not by Bread Alone
Technology
Green Revolution
The Invasive Species
Smarter, Stronger, Smaller
Neoagriculture: A Postscript

Flames in Farming
Meaning of Fire
Evolution of Fire Management
Sustainability
Fire in the Sky
Fire Down Below
Power for the People
Soul of Fire

# Preface

The following pages are about the human animal's relation to the planet. They focus on some features of human creativity and adaptability that have enabled mankind to survive, prosper, and expand. They also argue that mankind's commendable accomplishments have downsides, not the least of which has been the survival of extremely large numbers. So I will open our conversation with a passage from W.S. Merwin's poem, "The Gods:"[1]

"What is man that he should be infinite....On the door it says what to do to survive But we were not born to survive Only to live"

In this statement about human creations I mean more than inventions, though inventions are part of creation. Creation here is whole process, including "paradigm shifts," managed and manipulated by the human mind. As such the boundaries of creations are often indefinite, with shady beginnings and faded endings.

In the sense that all facts are historical, the creation stories contain some history. My intent, however, is not simply to report historical events or evolutions, but to argue for a purpose. Such is the posture taken by Friedrich Nietzsche in his "On the Advantage and Disadvantage of History for Life." While neither a student nor apostle of Nietzsche, I was captivated by his perspective of history which I believe attaches to most if not all dimensions of knowledge. He opened with "...our need for history is quite different from that of the spoiled idler in the garden of knowledge... we require history for life and action..." and he then asserted "Only so far as history serves life will we serve it." (Nietzsche, p 7) When humanity's pursuit of knowledge has purpose, creation is possible. Consider seven possibilities.

Why seven? Because seven seemed sufficient to describe the dimensions of human impact on Earth. Seven, of course, carries some symbolic freight such as the seven days of creation in the Bible, good and famine years in Pharaoh's dream, seven wonders of the world, seven wise men of Greece, and so on. Seven often symbolizes completeness or sufficiency, i.e., enough. During a review of this book's draft, one reader proposed government as another creation. Good idea, but after some discussion we concluded that "governance" was a feature of many, if not all, creations—the progression of all creations is subject to their governance. So we deemed "the seven" significant, not exhaustive, but a starting point.

The chapters are in a 3-3-1 formation. Chapters 1, 2, and 3–agriculture, fire, medicine– represent three human interventions in nature. Chapters 4, 5, and 6–money, logic, writing–represent human organization. Chapter 7, in the goalkeeper position, is about God, for explaining the unexplained.

The main points may be summarized briefly, beginning with agriculture. Agriculture's primacy in the order of creations stems from the need for food to sustain life. Success in food and fiber production not only assures survival but frees up resources to enhance civilization. But success in agriculture has come at the expense of increased dependency on human enterprise and decreased reliance on nature's benevolence and discipline.

Fire and energy management molded the equipment of modern man. From bronze battle axes to fiber optics, fire has defined the character of human dominance on earth. Once man could ignite and control fire and energy he rejected Malthusian cautions and claimed planetary regency through technology. Humans enlarged their numbers, expanded their desires, and extended their abilities to fuel their fires, while nature's role in the human condition receded and exposed its omen, pollution.

Medicine further improved mankind's ability to resist disease, repair damage of body or mind, and extend life expectancy. *Homo sapiens* now alive on Earth number 7 billion and growing, presenting the species with questions and problems that, so far, they have been unwilling to address. Human interventions in nature have had side effects such as pollution, degradation of resources, physical unfitness, war, dependence on human fixes of problems rather than nature's broadband (sometimes harsh) corrections.

Money is a clever device for moving, storing, and representing value. It is the lubricant of trading relationships, a critical feature of economy. Hence, money in the economy was selected as a metaphor for all features of an organized society. As in all creations, it is evolving and does not always serve everyone equally or justly, or sometimes at all.

Writing appears not only on money but everywhere. What we recognize as writing has been around for 5 millennia, or about half the time of agriculture, but its service has been critical. Civilization would seem impossible without writing, as the means for conveying ideas long distances and storing information for long times. Perhaps most critical in the creation process is writing's quality of retention, that is, an idea or message when committed to writing is less subject to alteration or nuance, and hence subject to evaluation—detection, reflection, correction.

Nature bestowed humans with two formidable gifts—a brain and two thumbs. The thumbs helped make and use tools. The brain enabled thinking, and then, thinking about thinking or, Logic.

Logic is the latest of mankind's creations, expressed here, albeit arbitrarily, with Aristotle's syllogisms. The syllogisms are a set of rules to yield valid conclusions from well-formed premises.

However, just as two thumbs are no assurance against fumbling or misusing a tool, logic alone is no assurance against nonsense. Logic may be necessary, but not sufficient.

Mysteries and befuddlements are features of the human condition. New knowledge gives rise to new unknowns. The unknown, the uncertain, the worrisome, beset the human animal. As nature abhors a vacuum, humans abhor unanswered questions. One answer to the unknown is God, whose existence can be rendered workable with the concept of "as if."

Two key notions repeated throughout are, first, that increases in the sum of knowledge do not reduce doubt and uncertainty but rather increase the awareness of more areas of ignorance. Second, that creation is a continuing process of detection, reflection, correction. Even God miscalculates, ponders, and then fixes.

As Copernicus and Galileo revealed that Earth was part, not the pivot, of the universe, I accept humans as part, not the pivot, of life on Earth. I do not accept that Earth's creatures and features exist to serve humans, but that they (we) are part of a cooperative enterprise and, further, that failure to cooperate will have serious, e.g., non-survival, consequences. Failure of humans to control their own numbers, for example, has already produced negative consequences or, to say the least, sub-optimal conditions.

The book is intentionally compact, meant to be a greeting, not a last word. These seven creation stories attempt to understand and explain the world and universe of which we are a part. They are expressions of concern and hope. Humanity's most valuable resource is knowledge, the stuff of creations. The reader is invited to share in the production, exchange, and conservation of that knowledge.

I am indebted to countless persons for the benefits of their thoughts, arguments, writings, conversations, and stimulations. However, a few must be acknowledged separately and specially. Former coworker in USDA's Economic Research Service, Clark Edwards, was particularly helpful in the early stages of writing. Dale

Simms employed his editorial skills thoughtfully and professionally. On some subjects such as population, I benefited not only by her expertise but the moderating counsel of my wife, Gooloo. I got many helpful comments and insights from Paul Barkley, John Marshall, Robert Nelson, and Paul Thompson. To all I am most grateful.

# Agriculture

Agriculture may rightly claim primacy among all human creations. Indeed, Jack Harlan opens his book, *The Living Fields*, by declaring that "All civilizations, from the earliest we know about down to our own, have evolved from an agricultural base ...and made our modern world possible" (Harlan. 1995, p. xiii). And Jared Diamond rests his story of human development on the foundation of agriculture: "...food surpluses, ...and the animal-based means of transporting those surpluses, were a prerequisite for the development of settled politically centralized, socially stratified, economically complex, technologically innovative societies" (Diamond, 1997, p. 92).

Agriculture embodies the essence of human creativity, namely, that as humans invent new technologies, they reinvent themselves. Those processes are revealed in the transition from hunting and gathering to farming and herding. Creation's interactive changes are complex. To illustrate that complexity, agriculture is a perfect place to start.

The manipulation of living things—plants and animals—for human benefit is the core feature of agriculture. It is called "domestication" to bring living things into the home, from whence the plant or animal is managed, from selection to genetic modification,

1

to serve the human purpose. But domestication is a two-way street. Human physiology, health, habits, and ideas are shaped by the relationship. David Rindos, in the context of evolution, for example, elaborates on the idea of domestication as "modes" or stages—incidental, specialized, and agricultural. Creation through domestication takes time.[2]

Agriculture occupies a small fraction—about 10,000 years—of the 150,000 years or so that *Homo sapiens* has existed. Anthropologists and archaeologists struggle to pinpoint both of these numbers. Still, compared to the life of the planet and its cavalcade of creatures, both mankind and agriculture are newcomers. Productivity, as measured by the number of persons supported by each person engaged in agriculture, has skyrocketed only in the last century or less.

## In the Beginning Was the Dog

Domestication began with mankind's relation to *Canis lupus familiaris*, long before the origins of farming and herding. The hunting of prey and the guarding of "gatherings" began the partnership of man and dog. Domestication, or domination, was but an extension of *Homo sapiens'* alpha position in the pack.

The relationship between humans and dogs began in the Paleolithic or Mesolithic era, at least distant enough in time to be controversial among scientists. It was once commonly thought that dogs were domesticated before the peak of the last ice age, as much as 40 millennia ago. Some recent DNA studies propose a more recent date, about 15,000 years ago in east Asia.

Dogs bridge the cultural gap between hunter/gatherer and agriculturalist. Dogs first applied their pack instincts to the human-directed roles of guards, protectors, and hunting companions before being enlisted as herders, carriers, and draft animals. Dogs, in other words, were partners in the creative evolution of agriculture. Over time, dogs evolved into special breeds designed to find and kill rodents, or protect and herd other domestic (meat) animals. Their canine senses, speed, strength, endurance, and courage enabled dogs to reduce predations on provisions, crops, and domestic animals. In return, the humans provided dogs a steady supply of food, some shelter, and rudimentary medical care. The significance of dogs belies the notion that agriculture is solely a human creation, or that it emerged fully formed in a "eureka" moment and not by degrees over longs stretches of evolutionary time.

A traditional classification of farm animals would emphasize sheep, goats, llamas, camels, cattle, swine, and horses. Of these, the first farm animals to be domesticated were sheep,[3] at about the same era (9,000 to 11,000 years ago) and in roughly the same place (northern Iraq) as wheat and other cereals. Sheep were kept as a moveable, reliable source of meat and pelts. Not until other technology was sufficiently advanced, 5,000 years later, did wool and weaving extend the full value of sheep to humans.

Domestication of these animals reflects a symbiotic relationship. In exchange for food and shelter, agricultural animals provide humans with a supply of food, clothing, and draft energy. Over time, humans engineered animals to better suit human purposes. Specialized breeding has produced designer sheep fleece or pelt qualities, meat or milk production, and adaptability to regional conditions. Sheep are now found in all parts of the world, but they tend to favor more arid regions. Countries with the most sheep are China, Australia, and India, in that order. The Food and Agriculture Organization reported that the number of sheep in 2003 was over 1 billion worldwide. The number of sheep, goats, cattle, and other grazing animals is causing great concern about overgrazing. Like humans, their number is probably unsustainable ecologically.

## Settlement and Agriculture

The origins of agriculture are conventionally dated circa 10,000 years ago (8,000 BCE) and attributed to a region known as the fertile crescent of the Middle East. In fact, primitive agriculture is much older if its origins are aligned with early domestication of animals. Plants may have grown incidentally alongside human settlements, and then intentionally by rudimentary planting and nurturing.[4] Following the last principal ice age, human cultural, organizational, and technological changes were underway in Europe and the Middle East that would both require and enable the domestication of plants and animals. Cauvin describes pre-agricultural villages of the Natufian era, 12,500 to 10,000 BCE, "the pivotal period when the process of neolithisation was prepared...[during] which human communities passed from hunting and gathering to the production of their subsistence base" (Cauvin, 2000, p.15). Archeological research indicates that this development took place throughout the entire Levant, but with variation from Mediterranean settlement inland toward the Euphrates or toward the Negev. The Natufian economy rested on a "very eclectic strategy" in collecting wild foods, including wild cereals.

The size and location of human agglomeration was clearly dictated by the nearness and abundance of plants and animals that nature, unaided, could provide. The expansion of sedentary settlements both required and enabled agriculture.

Domesticated plants, being less mobile, had a larger and more immediate bearing on the growth of villages and cities than herds of domesticated animals.[5]

## Grasses and Other Plants

For omnivore *homo*, plants comprise a large portion of the food intake. Plants are in dazzling variety, such variety that humans can have wholesome diets eating vegetables only. These plants include the cereals such as wheat, barley, and rice; fruits such as bananas, strawberries, and apples; tubers like potatoes, carrots, and yams; and nuts such as cashews and coconuts. The grasses include sugar cane from which the sweetener is extracted, and bamboo yielding edible sprouts and building material. Other plants provide condiments, textile fibers, medicines, and decorations. The level of domestication may range from the collection of pharmaceutical plants in the wild[6] to laboratory modification of genetic structure.[7]

In the human struggle to ensure a reliable source of nutrition, the cereals have played an important role, even before agriculture. The seeds of grasses were not only nutritious, but portable, storable, and durable. Grains could sustain life over the seasons, and during times of crisis. Durability and storability were features supporting settlement, protection, cultivation, selective breeding, and other inventions of domestication, or agriculture. The human population's sustenance depends heavily on three grasses—wheat, corn, and rice. Without them, even one of them, much of the world's population would starve.

Ancestors of the common or bread wheat were wild grasses, einkorn and emmer. Some hybridization in the wild enabled, biologically, the development of modern bread wheat. Wild einkorn relics have been dated to 12,000 years ago (10,000 BCE) in the Near East. Modern versions of this cereal are still grown in Europe and India. Einkorn is superior to common bread wheat in its protein, fat, and (some) mineral content, though its baking qualities are inferior to modern bread wheats. The family of relic wheats—emmer, einkorn, spelt, and triticale—regardless of niche appeals, is clearly inferior in productivity and will likely remain inconsequential as a world food resource compared to common bread wheat and durum. Domestication has resulted in the highly productive wheat, a wheat that is genetically complex[8] and no longer capable of supporting itself in the wild.

Some 9,000 years ago in the Near East, the first appearance of a predecessor of today's common bread wheat coincided with the origins of agriculture.[9] Wheat's long history virtually defines agriculture. It has been the staple of human diet throughout the world and, to a large extent, has supported the growth of human population.

Dating of wheat origins and domestication remains controversial among archeobotanists, but Nesbitt (2001) posits that domestication of wheat and its predecessors came about in different places and at different paces. In the mid-19th century, for example, excavations in Switzerland revealed einkorn, emmer, and spelt, as well as three hexaploid (bread) wheats. Later studies in the Swiss excavations showed that the hexaploids were, in fact, tetraploids (today's pasta wheats).

Over millennia, wheat farming likely evolved via selection from among nature's mutations and hybrids; aided by mechanical technology such as metal implements, irrigation, and animal power; and mindful of the relative productivity, storability, and palatability of particular strains of wheat. As a rough measure of wheat's evolution, the wild einkorn and goat grass of 30,000 BP hybridized to wild emmer, then cultivated emmer hybridized with a goat grass descendant about 9000 BP to produce spelt. After 8500 BP, a descendant of cultivated emmer evolved into *triticum durum* (pasta) wheat and spelt evolved into *triticum aestivum* (bread) wheat. Mideast wheat creations were duplicated in Africa and what is now Europe.

Varieties of wheat number in the hundreds, many adapted to suit special uses, for resistance to diseases, for growing in difficult conditions such as high salinity, and for hardiness in rain, cold, or drought. Broadly defined, there are six types of wheat classed by season of planting and qualities of the grain: Hard Red Winter and Hard Red Spring, both bread wheats high in protein; Soft Red Winter and Soft White used for cakes and pastries low in protein; Hard White used for hard rolls, bulgur, and tortillas; and Durum, a pasta wheat grown predominantly in North Dakota.

The botanical roots of maize are controversial, but most hypotheses posit teosinte either as the sole primitive ancestor or contributor to a hybrid subspecies. Some early versions of maize were very small, about 2 inches long. The wide variety of large cobs now include sweet corn, popcorn, dent corn, and flint corn. Maize has been a staple of the Americas for thousands of years and worldwide for 500 years.

Domestication of maize, or an immediate maize predecessor, appears to have occurred about 7500 BP in central or south Mexico (Harlan, 1995, p. 177; Heiser, 1990, p. 96). That would date the farming of maize in the Americas roughly in the same era as the first farming of wheat in the Middle East. Maize found its way to Europe shortly after Spanish invasion of the Americas in the 15th century, and wheat arrived in the Americas from Europe with settlement in the 16th century.

Generally, maize (or corn) requires a more temperate and moist climate than wheat. In addition to food for humans and livestock, maize is used for industrial products such as starch, sweeteners, and oil. It is used more than wheat and rice for livestock feed, either as grain or ensilage.[10] Like the other cereals, maize requires intense fertilization, pest and weed management, disease control, and horticultural research and design. In early 2008, the corn genome had been completely mapped, enabling humans to further manipulate this plant to resist insects and diseases, and redesign the plant's growth requirements and productivity. *Zea mays* is no longer fashioned by nature's forces; it, too, has become merely an extension of *Homo sapiens.*

Rice, *Oryza,* is the basic food for more than half the world's population. Its water, climate, and labor requirements have limited its range. "The archaeological record of rice is far inferior to that of wheat, but present evidence indicates that it was in cultivation in both India and China before 5000 B.C." (Heiser, 1990, p. 81). At 7000 BP, the domestication of rice occurs roughly in the same era as wheat and maize. Nutritionally, rice is seriously inadequate, especially when it is hulled to convert brown rice into white rice. Diets of rice are improved by the addition of vegetable protein from soybeans or animal protein from fish raised in the paddies.

All the cereals in their early domestication were heavily influenced by nature. Then, human domination gained precedence through selection, controlled fertilization and cultivation, and eventually scientific plant breeding and genetic modification. Still, without the grasses—notably the big three of wheat, maize, and rice—the human population and its dependent animal population would be but small fractions of their present numbers, perhaps even extinct.

## Not by Bread Alone[11]

There is more to the agriculture story than food. While food is a good proxy for the emergence of farming from picking, grubbing, and hunting, it is not the complete tale of human interventions in growing plants and animals. Food is essential for life, but coverings for humans'delicate skin, and shelter from the elements also are needed. Fiber in a wide variety of forms—silk to timber—are basic ingredients of the coverings and containers figured in human survival and comfort.

Pelts protected humans from chill winds and prickly thorns long before agriculture existed and continued to serve human uses in the transition from hunter-gatherer life.[12] Many of the techniques of processing, preserving, and joining the skins of hunted animals were adopted and adapted to herded animal skins. Leather still occupies a significant niche in the human coverings economy, much of it the byproduct of other animal uses. Jackets, coats, gloves and shoes are to this day made from animal skins.[13] Some animal hides and furs are regarded as items of fashion, supporting a sub-form of agriculture, e.g., mink farms.

The origins of wool fabric are uncertain and surrounded by mythology, but wool products were in use in Neolithic and Bronze ages. Most likely, wool attached to the hide, e.g., shearling, was worn before fabrics were made from shorn wool by felting, weaving, or knitting. Earliest wool fabric probably was felt which relies on the naturally cohesive qualities of the outside surfaces of the wool hairs when combed, cooked, rubbed and pressed together. Uses of felt vary from the tent-like yurts in Central Asia to slippers, boots, auto parts, and musical instruments. More commonly, wool becomes fabric by weaving, that is, crossing wool warp threads at right angles to weft threads on looms dated from as early as 5000 BCE to 2000 BCE.[14]

While leather and wool played their roles of durability and protection, the slender filaments of the silk worm played to refinement and luxury. Among the smallest of agricultural animals, the silk worm has served humans for at least 4000 years. Sericulture originated in China and was a closely held secret for hundreds of years, finally migrating West through Japan, India, and Egypt by 200 CE. Silk worm raising, silk reeling, and silk weaving was not established in southern Europe until the 11th century, and attempted in England as late as the 17th century.[15]

Fibers originate from both animal and plant sources. A fragment of woven fabric was discovered in Cayonu, Turkey, and carbon dated to 9000 years ago, that is, in the earliest stages of the agricultural age when residents of that site were still mixing hunter-gathering and agricultural living. The fabric at the Turkey find was linen and there was some evidence of getting both oil and fiber from the flax.

Cotton was cultivated at least 8000 years ago in Mexico. It was a descendant of a wild form which, through agriculture, enlarged its boll and lengthened its staple. Cotton also was cultivated in the Indus valley around 7000 years ago, with spinning and fabrication substantially advanced by the 3rd century BCE. Cotton was slow to catch on in Europe--not until the 17th century did Great Britain develop a cotton fabrication industry based on imports from India and the Americas. Cotton's production and trade has been an important influence on many nations' culture and politics, witness British hegemony in 18th-19th century India and Egypt, and the culture and politics of the American south.

Today cotton is the world's leading natural fiber with an annual production of 114 million bales harvested on 32 million hectares.[16] Cotton, pure and blended, has provided essential cover for human migration and civilization.

Plants provide fuel, pharmaceutical, textile, construction, and other products useful for human survival and well-being. Fiber from the papyrus plant in Egypt was pressed into paper-like sheets to become the writing surface of choice in 3rd millennia Egypt. Hemp has provided cordage for Egyptians since the 4th millennia BCE and there is indirect evidence of hemp cloth (impressions in clay) found in pre-agricultural Turkey 9th millennia BCE. Hemp varieties supply building materials, textiles, paper, medicines, biodegradable containers and a growing number of products and its cultivation is environmentally friendly.

Wood is an organic analog to iron—abundant and versatile for making things. In particular, wood, in a variety of forms, is used in building shelter. Sticks and poles woven together and plastered with clay produce a wattle and daub house. Logs laid atop of one another produce a log cabin. Sawed and planed lumber is joined easily for frames and roofs to provide shelter almost anywhere. Forestry has tailored the types of trees, and the methods of growing and harvesting timber to meet demands of an ever enlarging population. About a third of the world's land surface is forested and the development, management, and preservation of woodland represent prominent dimensions of agriculture. Forests, like fields and flocks, yield to agriculture's dominating technology.

## Technology

The emergence of agriculture from a nature-driven hunter-gatherer culture was very likely slow, exploratory, and piecemeal. The first farmers observed plants in nature as the basis for selective breeding, seedbed selection and preparation, fertilization, watering, and harvesting.

Selective breeding apes the natural processes of evolution—surviving varieties endure or prosper under prevailing moisture, disease, and nutritional conditions. Human creativity consists of bending the evolutionary process toward the needs and wants of humans. The plants with productive and taste qualities suited to humans will be selected and nurtured, with competition plants weeded out.

Seedbed locations may have been chosen to mimic nature. Hunter-gatherers, after all, knew where to look for food and would carry their horticultural wisdom into plant domestication. In the earliest stages of agriculture, much of the planting may have been accidental or unintentional. Observation and association was followed by trial and error. Early placement of seeds factored in cultivator's access and safety on top of the plant's preferred setting. Plants tended by humans would survive and prosper, but grow dependent on human care.

Tillage enabled the cultivated plant's roots to expand and access nutrients for growth. Tillage also enabled the cultivator to eliminate some of the cultivated plant's competition for nutrients and water. First tillage consisted of breaking the soil with stick, stone, or skeletal tools. Harlan describes the digging stick in great detail, and notes that in some places it is still used.[17] Soil preparation was based primarily on human power until cattle were enlisted into agriculture some time before 5,000 BP, at about the halfpoint of agricultural history. Later, horses replaced oxen as draft animals at different locations and times around the world. Today, Asian bison, oxen, horses, and mules still perform important draft functions, including tillage.

Not until the 20th century did mechanical power replace animal power. Until late in the 18th century, soil was opened with crude wooden plows, smoothed with hoes and rakes, and seeded by hand. Crops were harvested with a hand sickle and threshed by flail or foot. In the 19th century, when slavery was abolished in the

United States, incentives for labor saving technology in agriculture were heightened.

Power from steam, then the internal combustion engine, drove the mechanical revolution in agricultural production. But not until well into the 20th century did mechanical power replace animal power in the major segments of commercial agriculture. In many farm regions of the world, animals remain the dominant source of power for agriculture. The practice of fertilization probably began as farmers observed nature, noting that plant growth was superior amid animal droppings, decaying vegetative matter, or human refuse. In some places, seasonal flooding provided leached minerals. For example, as early as 6000 BP, flooding along the Nile, Tigris, Euphrates, and Zagros rivers brought both nutrients and water to adjacent crops.

Human intervention in fertilization began when organic materials were saved, stored, and deliberately applied to enhance plant growth, probably millennia into the creation of agriculture. For at least half of the history of agriculture, animal manure has been deliberately applied to terraced fields.[18] Cultivation and fertilization were combined in the building of plaggen soils in peat-rich areas of Europe as long ago as the Bronze Age. Beginning in the 19th century, enormous quantities of guano from islands off Peru and the Caribbean entered into international trade as nitrogen- and phosphorus-rich fertilizer, and later in the 19th century, agriculture absorbed synthetic or inorganic fertilizers.

Water is an essential ingredient of life. Its management, therefore, is a benchmark of human dominance over plant and animal growth. The cereals vary widely in their water requirements as to quantity, frequency, and quality. Wheat grows well in relatively arid climates, whereas rice growth requires large volumes of water. There is some evidence of irrigation as long ago as 7,000 BP in Mesopotamia and Egypt and 6,000 BP in the Andes mountains of Peru.

Among the earliest adopters of water management were the Nile farmers who adjusted their cultivation practices to the seasonal flooding of the river. Water was stored in a natural lake for use during dry periods. Later, a large masonry dam was built to control Nile waters for irrigation.

The single factor now most likely to limit the ability of humanity to sustain itself (and its codependents) is water. Simply stated, "Water is life." While groundwater management is but one aspect of human manipulation of finite freshwater resources, it can serve as a proxy for water conservation generally. William Ashworth portrays the significance of groundwater elegantly in *Ogallala Blue:*

"Pumping the Ogallala dry will have consequences. It is necessary to understand these consequences, to mitigate them where mitigation is possible, and to figure out how we are going to live with them where it is not...springs dry up, rivers diminish, the numbers and varieties of plants and animals are reduced...increased food costs...bankruptcies, foreclosures, forced migrations, failed businesses, abandoned towns..." (Ashworth, 2006, pp. 11,12)

As mankind harnessed water to advance agriculture, settlements grew and technology advanced, as evidenced by bronze and iron tools, improved plows and seed drills, commercial milling, and presses for olive oil and grapes. In Mesopotamia around 5200 BP, the wheel was developed for transportation. The honey bee was domesticated about 4500 BP. Draft animals were enlisted to pull or carry the tools and products of agriculture, freeing up the time and muscle power of humans. Advances in agriculture enabled persons to turn their talents, time, and resources to activities other than hunting and gathering. Agriculture supported growing populations which, in turn, pressured farmers and herdsmen to select and nourish plants and animals with ever greater productivity. Nature lost more of its self-determination.

The expansion of the human population from 5 million in 10,000 BP, the beginning of agriculture, to 50 million in 1,000

CE was accommodated with seed and breed selection, irrigation, fertilization, and the extension of cultivated and grazed area. Two innovations—the moldboard plow and the horse collar, both originating in China—were crucial in agriculture's productivity spurt. The Chinese design of the horse collar distributed the pulling pressure away from the horse's trachea and onto the sternum and skeletal/muscular system. The collar and harness provided a direct line of traction to whatever was being pulled, greatly enhancing the power of horse[19] and redoubling the energy input to agriculture. Improvements in tillage instruments continue in agricultural industries throughout the world.

Some inventions were simple improvements of older ideas. The plow grew out of digging sticks and hoes. The first "plows" were pulled by humans. Metal plow tips and then whole iron plows magnified the productivity of draft animals. Jethro Tull designed a mechanical seed drill in 1701, then an inter-row cultivator to weed between the seeded rows, both machines drawn by animal power. John Deere in 1837 developed a stronger steel plow that became the standard for plow design and manufacture. The tractor steam engine of the mid-19th century[20] was eclipsed by the lighter, more flexible fossil-fuel engines of the late 19th and early 20th centuries.

Two significant innovations serving modern agriculture were the railroad and refrigeration. Railroads, and the transportation system generally, shortened the travel time between food/fiber production and consumers. Refrigeration, as a food preserver, enabled transport distances to lengthen. Fewer, more productive, farmers and herdsmen could provide food to more distant agglomerations of people now engaged in things other than agriculture.

The cultural and political conditions for innovation were created in the Age of Enlightenment in the 18th century[21]. Inquiry blossomed. Ideas breached the ancient barriers of belief and tradition. Discoveries in biology, chemistry, and engineering would unravel many of nature's mysteries. On the basis of chemical analysis by Justus Liebig in the mid-19th century, an inorganic fertilizer industry made possible huge increases in agricultural productivity. The limitation of natural fertility was overcome, and crops became more dependent on human management.

A milestone in modern agriculture was Gregor Mendel's study of the inheritance of pea characteristics in the mid-19th century. From his research grew the science of genetics and genome analyses. James Watson, Francis Crick, and Maurice Wilson solved the mystery of how genetic characteristics were coded and transmitted. The basis for genetic modification was revealed and, with the aid of modern computer technology, plants and animals can now be engineered to specification. Less than one century passed between the two GMs—Gregor Mendel and genetic modification.

Significant changes in the engineering and management of agriculture were supported by institutional, cultural, and educational developments. President Abraham Lincoln, in 1862, signed legislation creating the Land Grant College system, the Department of Agriculture, and the Homestead Act.[22] The Homestead Act distributed the people's land to those who would live and produce on it. Land Grant Colleges extended advanced learning to ordinary people. The Department of Agriculture expanded and improved the people's capacity to provide primary goods of food, fiber, and shelter.[23]

## Green Revolution

In this past century, the growth of human population has presented agriculture with enormous challenges. One example of how that challenge was confronted has been labeled the "green revolution," personified by Norman Borlaug.[24] In the late 1940s, the Government of Mexico and the Rockefeller Foundation initiated research to increase Mexico's wheat growing capacity in the face of a large and growing population. Wheat farmers were losing wheat yield to stem rust. The wheat was subject to lodging because of its length and weakening by rust. By the 1960s, Borlaug's breeding program had produced a shorter stemmed, disease- resistant, wheat that was higher yielding. The improved strains of wheat were further developed for greatly expanded production. The breeding techniques were exported to other countries and applied to other plants, notably maize and rice. The "green revolution" arose from plants that were stronger, smaller, and with a more productive head.[25]

## The Invasive Species

For up to two-thirds of the total time *Homo sapiens* have existed, that is up until 70,000 years ago, our number hovered at around 2,000.[26] By the beginning of agriculture—10,000 to 8,000 years ago—the number of humans had grown to 5 or 10 million. By then, humans occupied, more or less, the entire planet. By the time Vikings first landed in North America, circa 1000 CE, there were over 300 million humans.[27] Forces of nature—the diseases of plants, humans, and other animals; drought, floods, insects, and earthquakes—were so successfully overcome by the genius of humans (and luck) that by 2000 CE the planet supported over 6 billion people. By 2020, less than half a generation hence, the number of people, as projected by the U.S. Bureau of Census, will be near 8 billion.

Meanwhile the space on planet Earth has remained constant. No part of Earth remains untouched by some human influence, but the density of occupation varies widely.[28] Total surface of the planet is 197 million square miles. About 29 percent of the planet's surface is land, amounting to 58 million square miles. However, much of that land (deserts, ice, mountains, etc.) is uninhabitable without extreme technological support. The area of arable land might be expanded slightly, but the current 12 million square miles is about the limit with foreseeable technology.[29] Much of that arable land is adjacent to a major river such as the Nile, Ganges, or Mississippi, highlighting the importance of water in the future of agriculture and life generally. In short, Earth's allotment of space and fresh water is now fully subscribed, and any additional resources carved out by agriculture or for competing demands will come at substantial cost.

Among the challenges besetting agriculture even in the near term is its dependence on water. Although 70 percent of the surface of the earth is covered with water, only about 2.5 percent of the water is fresh, with more than half of that held in polar ice caps and glaciers. Freshwater in lakes and streams, available for human use, is less than a half of 1 percent. Agriculture is estimated to account for 70 percent of freshwater use.[30] It is no surprise that drought is a serious problem for crop and livestock production, but also for human consumption. Even where water is relatively abundant, agriculture is in sharp competition with industry and household use.

The productivity of agriculture enabled fewer persons to supply food and fiber in such abundance that they and others had time and energy to invent, construct, transport, and trade. The agglomerations of people grew as the capacity of agriculture to grow and transport food expanded. Urbanization was made possible by the increased ability of farmers to feed the cities.[31] Today there are over 100 cities in the world with over 3 million people.[32] In the language of modern agriculture, cities are CAFOs (confined animal feeding operations), totally dependent on the flow and restocking of agricultural products, with waste a source of contention and concern.

The growth of the human population may not be due to agriculture, but agriculture clearly made growth possible. Recall Richard Cantillon's observation that "men tend to reproduce like mice in a barn," unless contained by some powerful force, such as famine or plague.[33] About 50 years later, the Reverend Robert Malthus published an *Essay on the Principle of Population*. Malthus' thesis was that food shortage was one of the natural checks on population, a thesis parsed and argued by academics and others to this day. Those who insist on proving Malthus wrong cite the remarkable success of agriculture. But therein is the danger. Because agriculture has been so adept in feeding large numbers of people, other challenges have emerged. Huge energy demands have drawn down the stocks of resources. The supply of fresh water is evaporating. Forest and grasslands are retreating, along with the wildlife they support. Environmental hazards such as global warming are growing.

Another critical influence on the character of the human species is its connection to a diversity of living forms. E.O. Wilson in his book, *The Creation,* appeals for the preservation of diversity of life on Earth:

> "Humanity must make a decision, and make it right now: conserve Earth's natural heritage, or let future generations adjust to a biologically impoverished world. There is no way to weasel out of this choice."[34]

Perhaps the least recognized problem of unrestrained human reproduction is simply the loss of space and the effect of that loss on our character. Space, as the embodiment of freedom, openness, and opportunity, informs our spirituality and underpins any instinct toward "stewardship"[35] of the Earth and its species.

The unpleasant presence of too many people is not directly an agricultural issue but a condition born out of agriculture's success. Humans now occupy or control all of Earth with the capacity to thwart all challenges to their dominance of the natural environment. Or so it appears at the moment. Agricultural science continually confronts the mysteries of life. The emergence of some new deadly plague or food destroying microbe is a constant threat. Science, management, and engineering must be prepared for the unexpected and the malevolent.

Humans can no longer partner with nature in ecological matters. Nature has largely ceded its role, and mankind might be loath to surrender its willfulness regarding animal and plant design and endurance. For good or bad, people are in charge, so the planet's future will depend on human intelligence and initiative. Unfortunately, at present, no Norman Borlaug has stepped forward.

## Smarter, Stronger, Smaller

The domestication that has encompassed so much of the living world has not yet been applied to the human species. Indeed, the notion of downsizing our appetites or numbers is met with charges of population control and eugenics.[36] Yet, even the most casual observer realizes that the sheer number of people and their rapacious consumption is having serious impacts on the nature of planet Earth. The environmental movement has endorsed a wide variety of ways to change human behavior to benefit the environment, like auto efficiency standards, smokestack emission reductions, recycling, and sustainable power sources. Each of the countless measures may buy the planet a bit more livability or sustainability, but their incremental effects have been quickly swamped by increased numbers. And advances that improve the quality of life and longevity of people, unquestionably desirable by themselves, compound the population effect. Apart from policing our own population growth, are there characteristics of the human species that might make our habitation of earth more benign? Perhaps "smarter, stronger, and smaller" would be a beginning.

In humans, "smarter" means extending the quality that most ensured the early survival and success of our species. Humans achieved dominance by their ability to solve problems, to imagine, to formalize thought processes, to seek truth. Smart includes, but is not limited to, intelligence. It also includes learning, discernment, wisdom, imagination, and other features of brainpower. The evolution of smart is education, the prime quality of human development.

"Stronger" means the physical capability of the human organism to resist disease, stress, deprivation, and other challenges to health and longevity. Human strength arises from the inner qualities of body without dependence on the care and aids we think of as medicine and medical science. Strength might include physical power, but strength is vitally those elements contributing to well-being. Strength might be thought of as the economy of well-being: fewer resources needed by the human body to carry on.

As a species, "smaller" means a lesser draw on the host environment.[37] This view of smaller was ably crafted by E.F. Schumacher[38] as "Buddhist economics" nearly four decades ago, and is the basis of much of today's environmentalist message. That message includes fewer people, and has been extended to human physical structure by Samaras and others noting that "...human height and weight have a much larger impact on our lives than is usually recognized...very large increases in food, water and raw materials are required to support a larger body size during one's lifetime...whether the world with 6 billion large or 6 billion small people has an enormous impact on resources and the environment" (Samaras, 2007, p. 1).

In sum, the story of agriculture is a narrative of human evolution and creativity. It can be told as change in the relationship between man and nature, the emergence of domestication. Domestication meant, and means, dominance over other species, and with that dominance much of Earth's circumstance.

In the story of agriculture, there is good news and bad news. The good news is that agriculture's production of food and fiber enabled the population of people to reach 7 billion. The bad news is that by disabling nature's firm, albeit harsh, check on population growth, the number of humans is 7 billion and growing. The human population is already incompatible with the planet's space and other species, and growth projections threaten even more. Humans are challenged to exercise the same control over themselves they wield over everything else. Agriculture is part of that challenge.

Despite the amazing advance in knowledge about the designs of life on earth, much remains uncertain, mysterious. And that mystery fires the advance of agriculture.

## Neoagriculture: A Postscript

Agriculture, at first the next logical step from hunter-gatherer culture and now a food and fiber colossus, has perhaps reached full development. Nature—climate, weather, water, pathogens, and mutations—still provides limits and challenges to the agriculturist. But food and fiber production has become so dominated by, and dependent on, human manipulation that agriculture is no longer an "intervention" but a requirement. McKibben (1989) called it "the end of nature."

The penultimate phase in agriculture's progression from human intervention in, to human replacement of, nature was launched, with the announcement in May 2010, of synthetic, computer-composed, DNA in a cell capable of self replication. It means the creation of life with no genetic ancestors.[39] This application of synthetic biology still required a natural cell shell into which the computer-generated DNA was inserted, but one is free to guess how long it will be before the shell, too, can be synthesized. Theoretically at least, synthetic biology could enable mankind to tailor-make organisms to suit any perceived need.

Economies and societies that are heavily reliant on nature for food and fiber are either small in number, materially impoverished, or both. The survival of the world's huge human population, much of it agglomerated into city CAFOs, depends completely on the often scorned "industrial agriculture."[40] With current population numbers and structure, the bucolic, closer-to-nature existence in developed economies will be an insignificant niche in the food and fiber sector.

Much of the world's increase in agricultural products will depend on a transfer of technology from developed countries to others. This is likely in part because research, experimental, and developmental capabilities are not available in low-income countries and because their growers are poor. Productive agriculture tends to be capital intensive, often at the expense of diversity. In the long run, transfer of high-productivity practices and species/subspecies may deplete the genetic base and increase vulnerability to monocultural dependencies, as E.O. Wilson warned (Wilson, 2006).

For ten millennia or so, human's purpose for agriculture has been to better feed, clothe, and shelter a growing population. But the planet's population of humans long ago exceeded numbers sufficient to sustain the species. Indeed, the numbers are so large as to threaten well-being, even survival. Perhaps another vision of agriculture is needed, one that includes both numerator and denominator in the materials/humans ratio. Bettering ourselves nutritionally and materially may require a focus not on extracting the most from food and fiber systems but on harnessing our best qualities as a species and reacquainting ourselves with simplicity and moderation. Malthusian equations need to address not just the narrow idea of food, but needs for space and other resources.

# Fire

The control, manipulation, and management of fire much preceded the arrival of *Homo sapiens*, the species of hominin accepted here as modern humans. According to Lockwood, "The use of fire is perhaps the most important innovation during the era of *H. Erectus*." (Lockwood, 2007, p.71) The long era of *Homo erectus* extended from about 2 million years to 200,000 years ago, overlapping several successor hominins, including perhaps early *Homo sapiens*. Among the first important uses of fire was cooking food. Members of *Homo erectus*, during much of their existence at least, were carnivores. Evidence of burned bones, dated 1 to 1.5 million years ago, has been found amid *Homo erectus* sites in southern Africa. And the sophistication of cooking would suggest even more elemental uses of fire, such as for warmth, defense against predators, and making tools such as spears. *Homo sapiens* inherited a substantial stock of knowledge about fire, so their creative contributions are often tied to other technologies. Modern humans were not the first creative users of fire, but did use fire in new, unique ways—including agriculture.

## Flames in Farming

Slash-and-burn practices are likely as old as agriculture itself. Indeed, burning as preparation for planting may date to the earliest inklings of agriculture. Some proto-agricultural practices may have occurred as opportunistic responses to natural or accidental fires. Budding farmers may have observed that planting in a scorched area was easier, that competitive plants (weeds) were controlled, and that ash enhanced fertility.

Rotational methods, in a variety of forms, have been one of the most durable practices in agriculture. The practice of clearing and burning native vegetation, followed by planting and growing, then fallowing, endures in some parts of the world. In lightly populated rain forest, slash-and-burn can be a practical, even sustainable, form of agriculture. However, sustainability requires that adequate natural cover be restored. The negative impacts of slash-and-burn occur when cleared erosive soils lose their fertility from excessive cropping and inadequate recovery. In western Madagascar, for example, the erosion from slash-and-burn agriculture is so severe that major rivers run red and the countryside appears to be bleeding.

By contrast, fire to power agriculture is a recent creation. Fire to make steam for mechanical power and to generate electricity spared enormous amounts of human and other animal energy. The internal combustion engine redoubled power gains in agricultural production and transport. By the mid-18th century, the first prototype steam engine was invented by James Watt, and its successors provided a wide range of stationary and, later, mobile applications.[41] In 1901, the first gasoline-powered farm tractor produced in scale was the Hart-Parr, designed by two agricultural engineers who gave it their names. In the 1930s, fuel-powered combine harvesters operated by a single person replaced stationary threshing machines operated by large crews. Small engines helped farmers move grain, pump water, and access electricity until supplied from an electrical grid in the mid-20th century. Agriculture joined other industries and consumers in burning the accumulated deposits of fossil fuels for power. Now, agriculture is supplementing fuel reserves with ethanol from maize, crop residues, switchgrass, and other sources of biomass.[42]

## Meaning of Fire

Fire, as flame in a lamp, transforms darkness into light. In the acetylene torch, it cuts and binds metal. In the firebox, it generates steam for mechanical or electrical power. Fire is indeed a mainstay of modern living.

The myriad uses of fire call for a fairly expansive definition.[43] The physics of fire, in simplest terms, is rapid oxidation, whereby fuel, heat, and oxygen undergo a sustained chemical reaction— combustion. Control of fire implies limiting one or more of these elements or interfering with the chemical chain reaction, as with a chemical fire extinguisher. If combustion is in a tightly confined area such as a lamp, fire box, or rocket, special arrangements may be required to provide sufficient air and fuel, or to confine or dissipate heat.

Flame appears when there is sufficient temperature and ignition, sustained as combustion. Temperatures rise and a chemical decomposition, pryolysis, takes place. When temperatures are sufficient, the fuel's char glows, air supports the combustion, and both fuel and gases from the fuel burn. Combustion produces heat energy.

Heat energy can also be generated by resistance to the flow of electrical current. Or inducted heat can be generated by molecular friction, as in a microwave oven. Electrical heat may also result from insulation leakage, gaps and arcing in broken power lines, static sparks, and lightning. Mechanical heat results from friction and is controlled with lubricating agents between the contacting or bearing surfaces. Heat is generated through compression, as in a diesel engine. Heat and radiation is released from the nucleus of an atom. Exploitation of all these sources is a relatively recent human endeavor. Many forms of "fire" have powered agriculture, industry, transportation, and the other dimensions of modern civilization.

## Evolution of Fire Management

The management of fire long preceded the ascendance of modern man, but its uses were primitive: warming, cooking, and fending off predators. In other words, the creative management of fire was stalled for a million years or so. Fire as a human tool made its next, and perhaps most significant, advance with the invention/discovery of ignition. Prior to their intentional ignition of fire, humans had to store and carry fire. Fire had to be tended by adding fuel or banking. Or fire had to be acquired from new sources, such as lightning or the coals of others.

Ignition was invented or discovered about the time agriculture began, somewhere around 10,000 years ago. Most likely, ignition started from the heat of friction caused by twirling a pointed wooden shaft into soft starter wood and dry tinder. Sparks from striking flint and pyrite came later. The creation of ignition extended the availability and flexibility of fire. However, aside from some agricultural practices, the uses of fire were confined to warming and cooking for several millennia. Emergence from the Stone Age changed all that.

The ability to start, stop, confine, and regulate fire complemented a number of other inventions; discoveries often achieve full fruition only through the arrival of another invention. Examples are smelting metals, firing bricks and pottery, and making or shaping glass. The craft and science of metallurgy was well underway before fire was added, upon which a great transformation in industry, society, art and warfare began.

The first metal to receive the attention of modern humans was gold.[44] Gold artifacts date from 8,000 years ago, or early in the development of agriculture and human settlement. The malleability of gold allowed it to be shaped by pounding, without firing. Then, as now, gold was used largely for jewelry or decoration. So was copper, until it was annealed, perhaps by accident in a camp fire.

There is no evidence of the intentional use of fire to reduce copper from free sources or minerals such as malachite before 4000 BCE. Smelting copper awaited a fire of at least 700°C (1292°F), a temperature attained in pottery kilns—another case of technology transfer, from pottery to metallurgy.

It took the discovery of tin, and its alloy with copper, to create a new era of civilization—the Bronze Age (from 3000-2000 BCE). The new metal, composed of 88 percent copper and 12 percent tin,[45] was stronger and more durable than copper, making it the true successor to stone as the instrument of a new civilization. Creating molten bronze requires temperatures of at least 925°C (1700°F). Fired bricks came into being about 5,000 years ago when larger, more sophisticated settlements had need for a stronger, more durable building material. Brickmaking was as old as permanent settlement, in turn made possible by agriculture. But fired bricks and pottery were needed for industry and commerce.

When higher temperatures were required to strengthen and glaze clay objects such as bricks and pottery, the kiln succeeded the open fire. The kiln enabled the brickmaker or potter to concentrate and regulate heat by controlling oxygen available to fuel. Bellows were added to this effect. A descendant of the kiln is the blast furnace.

Another metal and another age—Iron—is defined by fire (from 1800-1200 BCE) Iron is abundant on earth, but it melts at higher temperature than bronze. So despite its widespread availability in nature, it took improved fire management to be technologically and economically useful.[46] Iron's first implements and weapons were cast as wrought iron and, within 5 or 6 centuries, as steel. The steel with which the New World was conquered[47] was the result of progressively hotter fires—up to 800°C (1500°F)—carbon, and lots of hammering. Steelmaking techniques were in play perhaps 200 BCE in India, then migrated to Syria to become the renowned Damascus blades. Steel became the mass produced metal of industry in only the last millennium as Bessemer and other fire control techniques were developed.

Another significant development in metal shaping was wire. Although some ancient techniques were employed to create fine metal wires for jewelry and other decorative purposes, the large scale manufacture of wire for industrial and commercial uses did not come about until the 15th and 16th centuries. Wire was manufactured by drawing the heated metal through a sized aperture. In the 19th century, barbed wire became a significant tool in enclosing cattle and, in some circumstances, people. Perhaps most important is the role that wire of various metal compositions and sizes played in transmitting electricity and information.

Fire was at the heart of metallurgy and the higher temperatures required by iron and steel were attained with the use of charcoal. As the demands of construction, war, transportation, and food expanded, the demand for charcoal increased. Other inventions complemented metalworking. The wheel for pottery manufacture appeared around 7000 BP, for transportation around 5000 BP, with advances to spokes and bearings by 4000 BP. The wheel moved grain, people, wood, and charcoal. Charcoal fired the forges that made armaments,[48] ship parts, wheel tires, and better plows. Forests were cleared, areas denuded and eroded.

Eventually charcoal became scarce and coke derived from coal replaced it.[49] The story of steel and charcoal illustrates that advances in technology and industry are not costless. Although the soot and stench of coal, and later oil, have disgusted people for much of the Industrial Age, we have only recently become more fully aware of the environmental costs of burning fossil fuels.

Glass spans the existence of modern humans. Early glass, in the form of quartz, obsidian, and flint, was a product of nature, fired in the furnaces of deep earth and left in deposits for Stone Age people to fashion scrapers, slicers, and arrowheads. Quartz is an extremely abundant mineral, and appears in a wide variety of forms. Chemically, it is silicon dioxide, the predominant ingredient in glass. But it melts only at very high temperatures; only with the ability to marshal fires for extreme heat could glass become a feature of modern life. Pure silica, say crushed quartz or sand, melts at 2300 C (4200F) degrees but at lower temperatures when combined with other chemicals such as soda-ash and lime.

For about half the years from the beginning of agriculture, glass remained the product of nature. Obsidian and flint were the premium materials for Stone Age tools.[50] Then, about 5,000 years ago, humans added glazing to their pottery in overheated kilns. The earliest glass vessels have been dated at 3500 BP in Egypt, but glassblowing techniques appear unknown until the beginning of the Christian Era. Flat-glass production techniques emerged in the 12th century, with mass production of bottles and flat glass in the 19th and early 20th centuries.

The information technology revolution of the late 20th century incorporated glass and other fibers to transmit light signals, which are much faster than the electronic signals carried by metal wires. Glass used in optical cables is composed of nearly pure silica drawn to fibers finer than a human hair, under precisely controlled 1900° C (3452°F) heat.

Iron and glass are but two examples of the ingredients of modern technology made available to human manipulation by fire. Molten metal was shaped into engines for trains driven on rails of steel by steam. Then, fire in diesel engines generated electricity to power those trains. Fire in the engines of aircraft, ships, and autos have transformed industries, economies, societies, and the very character of humans, comforted against heat and cold behind barriers of clear glass. Molten sand has brightened and enlightened virtually every aspect of human life from lenses to light fixtures, from insulation to optical fiber. And somewhere, behind all the iron and glass, is fire. The management of heat and energy is fundamental to all aspects of human life. Small wonder that Empedocles[51] proclaimed fire as one of the four elements of nature.

## Sustainability

Nature has provided vast reservoirs of energy, discovered then exploited for the many features of human development. Throughout all but the most recent era, those reservoirs consisted of easily accessible wood and grass, then storable charcoal and peat. Coal has been burned for about two millennia, but on a large scale only since the industrial revolution. Petroleum and its distillates, kerosene and gasoline, were unavailable until the 19th century.

The fossil fuels–coal, petroleum, natural gas—are stock resources. That is, they are being replaced so slowly as to be considered finite. Exploration and exploitation of resources has become increasingly difficult and expensive. With the exponential growth in fossil fuel use by the developing world, the trend is unsustainable, and environmentally catastrophic.

More fire means poorer air, water, and earth. Sustainability and the tradeoffs between energy use and the environment are examined thoroughly in the massive text, *Sustainable Energy: Choosing Among Options* (Tester et al, 2005), which weighs on the importance of energy:

"The energy sector vastly exceeds all other industries in infrastructure size, capitalization, money transfer rates, and annual throughputs of raw materials and products....time scales for major technological innovations...are typically decades rather than years....complexity of the energy sector presents formidable challenges to rapid change" (p. 824).

Tester and company berate Rev. Malthus for overlooking the potential of technology (including energy) in his claim that human breeding would outrun food production. (p. 261). Of course, the food-producing technology of agriculture, including gasoline engines and petrochemicals, facilitated the population growth that now accounts for outsized energy demands. A broader perspective on Malthus would warrant a global or national population policy, at present nonexistent, to complement energy policy.

Although currently dominant as a source of energy, fossil fuels are not exclusive sources.[52] Two of nature's great sources of sustainable energy—one external, one internal—are the sun and earth's interior.

## Fire in the Sky

The sun's direct warmth and fuels of fire are an energy endowment to earth. The sun is widely regarded as the prime source of life. Its importance in the affairs of humans has endowed the sun with unsurpassed mythological and religious stature. A reasonable outcome of that regard is people's ongoing effort to capture some of the sun's power.

The great flaming ball at the center of our solar system is so large that it takes up all but a fifth of one percent of the total mass of the solar system. That bulk is sufficient to hold in its orbit all the other matter—including Earth—at substantial distances. Remoteness is fortuitous for Earth, because the surface of the sun is estimated at 5500°C (9900°F). Its content is almost three-quarters hydrogen and almost one-quarter helium, with a little oxygen, carbon, iron, and other minerals. The energy that supports life on Earth is generated by the sun's nuclear fusion of the hydrogen.

Solar energy is exploited for human use either directly as a source of heat or indirectly through photovoltaic electricity. The capture and focusing of the sun's rays to produce heat sustains people in desolate areas without other sources of fuel. Relatively simple, inexpensive devices cook food, and disinfect or distill water. Slightly more sophisticated parabolic reflectors can enlarge the capacity for generating heat, without pollution or toxicity. Shallow geothermal systems relying on the heat storing qualities of the soil can provide air heating and cooling. Photovoltaic cells can generate electricity for small scale and household purposes, and combined in sufficient quantity can supplement base-load generators.

Much of the planet's stored energy was the result of chemical processes, much as the next generation of solar energy will involve chemical engineering. Solar energy is used in producing hydrogen, for example. Ongoing research is exploring a wide variety of chemical uses of solar energy. But long before there were any researchers, or people for that matter, plants were drawing energy from the sun through the chemical process known as photosynthesis. Plants use sunshine and water to create carbohydrates from atmospheric carbon dioxide. A byproduct of this process is oxygen. We breathe only with the forbearance of plants and trees.

But the forests of the world are succumbing to human's rapacious clear-cutting for fuel, for building material, and for agriculture, displacing countless species of plants and animals. Clearly, human numbers and desires are overtaxing the forests that the sun alone cannot sustain.

## Fire Down Below

A short distance below the earth's surface nestles sufficient heat to serve almost all human energy needs. Temperatures rise in the descent toward the earth's core from about 1000° F at the boundary of the crust and outer mantle to 9000° F in the liquid outer iron core. The pressure responsible for this intense heat is so great that the inner core, about 1,500 miles in diameter, is solid. The core is primarily iron, but contains nickel, silicon, and potassium too.

From these depths issue the abundant mineral resources of iron and glass, two prime materials for human creations.

The outer boundary of the mantle, or base of the Earth's crust, ranges in depth from about 20 miles on land to 3 miles on the ocean floor. At those distances, subterranean temperatures range from 900° F to 1600° F. Earth's natural life is sustained by convection of fiery temperatures below contacting the empty cold of outer space. Life as we know it on the thin crust of earth functions in a narrow range between these two powerful forces. The more spectacular manifestations of this contact—warm springs, hot springs, and geysers—are found in many places around the earth, including "Old Faithful" in Yellowstone Park, and Geyser hot springs in Iceland. Their presence suggests the enormous potential of geothermal energy just a short distance from Earth's surface. The problem, of course, is that the technology to unlock that potential has thus far been limited, and more accessible fuels have deterred the engineering and commercial exploitation of geothermal energy.

Compared to the uses of fire by ancient hominins, or even the origins of agriculture, the technology for accessing the inner heat of Earth is very young, only about a century old. In Italy, at the beginning of the 20th century, the first electricity was generated from geothermal sources. Since then, the progress in geothermal has been relatively slow, and, despite great potential, supplies little of the world's energy except in Iceland.

Much of the current technology for the mining of heat resources rests on drilling techniques developed for the recovery of oil and natural gas. One hole is drilled into fractured hot dry rock (HDR) into which water is forced, superheated, and then recovered through another hole nearby. The superheated water or steam— 200°C (392°F) or more—drives generators on the surface to create electricity. Residual heat serves households and industries, and the cooled water is then circulated into the hot rocks below. Where

HDR fractures are not naturally sufficient to allow water to circulate, high-pressure techniques open up the rock fissures in much the same way oil and natural gas is recovered from waning fossil fuel fields.[53]

Research and development of enhanced geothermal systems (EGS) got underway in the 1970s, and working systems are producing electricity. The Massachusetts Institute of Technology has estimated that the energy in the EGS resource base of the United States, extractable with present technology, to be about 2,000 times the annual consumption of primary energy in the United States in 2005. The report adds: "With technology improvements, the economically extractable amount of useful energy could increase by a factor of 10 or more." (MIT, 2006, pp. 1-4) The EGS technology is sufficiently advanced as to be commercially viable now in the United States, Australia, and Germany. And this EGS technology is but a part of a larger operational, still larger conceptual, means for generating power from the earth's super-hot interior. With only modest support from government and industry geothermal development could in a relatively short time supply all electricity and heat needs.

What are the upsides and downsides of geothermal? For the shallow entries into the crust for heating and air conditioning there appear few if any drawbacks other than the cost of installation.[54] Evaluation of geothermal on large scale, therefore, pertains to electricity generation. Remarkably, the advantages of geothermal appear overwhelming, but not without some major shifts in how energy is supplied, used, and marketed. The downsides, therefore, are:

1. For many segments of transportation, fossil fuels and biofuels have greater portability. The bulk and short power life of electricity sources for motor vehicles translates into a disadvantage of geothermal. In transportation, geothermal awaits complementary improvements in power storage for electric engines.

2.  With current technology, some locations are relatively expensive either because of depth or underlying geological structure. Even with current technology, though, this cost is not overwhelming.

The upsides for geothermal appear far more convincing. Among those upsides are:

1.  Almost inexhaustible supply.[55] The MIT report on the Future of Geothermal Energy said that in the United States from an EGS reservoir of 13 million exajoules[56] an extractable portion of 200,000 exajoules in EGS would provide 2000 times all the energy we now use annually. Technology advances could extract much more.

2.  Geothermal provides a stable base-load supply of energy unaffected by the vagaries of wind, sun, or water reserves.

3.  Flexible plant scale and widespread location lowers power transmission costs.

4.  Widespread location also lowers the impact of hazards from natural or terrorist events.

5.  Geothermal doesn't require installation or maintenance of structures such as towers, solar panels, or refineries.

6.  Power is generated with virtually no pollution. Its constant base-load capacity complements other renewable sources of power.

## Power for the People

Throughout virtually all of their existence humans have relied on wood, grass, and other pickup combustibles to fuel their fires. Coal entered the industrial fuel picture in the 13th and 14th centuries, petroleum as kerosene in the mid-19th century. The first steam-powered locomotives were operational in England in 1803, were critical in the U.S. Civil War, and traversed a transcontinental track in 1869. Steam engines were fired by wood, then coal. Stationary steam engines were an important element in 19th and

20th century industrial development. Automobiles and gasoline refined from petroleum emerged in the late 19th century. Robust generation of electricity began with Edison's Manhattan project in the late 19th century. In short, power has become available on a large scale only in recent history.

The engines of economy and society are fueled largely by fossil fuels. Coal and petroleum are deposits formed millions of years ago from decaying organic matter under pressure and in sediment layers, a process that continues today but at rates insufficient to supply current demands. The supply, in other words, is being exhausted. Fossil fuels are the predominate source of energy. In the United States, for example, 83 percent of BTUs[57] consumed come from petroleum, natural gas, and coal. Since a fifth of Earth's energy consumption takes place in the United States (USDOE, EIA 2010 F14), that nation would seem to have a special responsibility for solving the energy shortfall and minimizing the environmental consequences of burning fossil fuels. Some opportunities appear promising.

Hydro and nuclear power plants have supplied electric energy in recent years. Nuclear plants now supply over 20 percent of America's electric power, and hydro generation less than 7 percent. Nuclear plants are subject to both security and environmental hazards. Much of the hydro potential in the United States has already been exploited.[58]

Currently, biofuel, solar, and geothermal sources of energy are receiving attention as alternatives to fossil fuels, although their current contribution to America's energy consumption is minimal. Biofuels are expensive, and emit much the same pollution in production and use as fossil fuels. Biofuels also draw upon agricultural resources. While not without some advantages over fossil fuels, it is unlikely that biofuels will improve significantly the current supply or quality of transportation and industrial energy.

Both wind and solar power have some potential, particularly with improved technology. Both can supply complementary power to other base-load sources, but they come up short—if the sun don't shine, and the wind don't blow.

Both present some aesthetic shortcomings, and structures require investment and maintenance expenses.

At varying costs, geothermal extractions and generators could be widely placed, lowering the costs of electricity transmission and minimizing the risks of failure from natural or manmade hazards. Startup technology is already available, and the course of improved engineering is easily envisioned. Geothermal is nearly pollution free. No structures. No transportation of fuel inputs. As such, geothermal appears to be the power source of the future.

At the opening of the 21$^{st}$ century, fabricating, distributing, maintaining the goods for, and providing the services of, modern economy is relying increasingly on electronics and electricity. Human energy and manipulation is being displaced by robotics and "additive manufacturing," Appliances, for example, can be customized and produced on demand, thus reducing the need for inventories and large scale model changes. Workers need not be concentrated in centralized workplaces. Less but more skilled labor will be needed. Humans will become a design force, not an energy source.

## Soul of Fire

Not surprisingly, fire has been held in awe throughout human evolution. Its power has been harnessed to serve humans in countless ways. Indeed, fire in its many forms has virtually defined civilization. Ancient philosophers proclaimed fire as one of the four basic elements of nature. Fire has served as a vital tool in artistic and scientific creation. Fire was a crucial feature of many religious traditions and rituals. The religion formed from the teachings of the prophet Zarathustra, for example, uses fire to symbolize "the divine spark that burns in each individual enlightenment and truth."[59]

Civilization is marked by the human ability to feed itself and direct energy toward its desired ends. When human energy was insufficient—or sufficiently unpleasant—human creativity mobilized fire for those desired ends– such as keeping warm, clearing farmland, glazing pottery, melting metals, making glass, powering machines, sending messages, travelling, learning. No longer dependent on nature's lightning to provide the gatherers of fire with warmth and protection, humans survived and thrived in greater numbers by their own ingenuity. Humans have enlarged their numbers, expanded their desires, and extended their abilities to fuel their fires, with both good and bad consequences.

The good news is that the power of sun and earth has made possible the growth and sustenance of 7 billion people. The bad news is that the resources of sun and earth have been ruthlessly exploited by people to grow their numbers to the bloated 7 billion.

The biological humans that evolved under the hardships of nature prospered when those strictures were overcome by wit and cunning. But those very survival instincts, unchecked by nature, meant an overwhelming expansion in population. Thus far, humans seem incapable or unwilling to apply that wit and cunning to manage their own numbers.

# Medicine

The clever survival abilities of *Homo sapiens* are undermined by the limits on durability. Humans are breakable, their parts malfunction, they host parasites and diseases, and they wear out and die.

As humans created agriculture for a larger, more reliable supply of food, and managed fire to stay warm, make tools, and build things, humans intervened in nature's flow of afflictions. Humans learned how to fix broken bodies, cure disease, prevent disease, relieve pain, and even delay death—slightly.

Under the heading "medicine" is a broad spectrum of interventions in nature's distresses of bodily health and longevity. Surgery, drugs, tests, manipulation, diet, and counsel are included in the arsenal of interventions. Roots of medical practice extend back well before *Homo sapiens,* but the traditions and advances of medical creativity can best be illustrated by events of the modern (agriculture) era, especially in more recent years.

## Early Times

Tissue deteriorates and scatters, so evidence of health conditions in ancient times is limited. Archeologists are able to infer some health problems from bones, but the supposition of other conditions and treatments must be based on unusual finds and considerable imagination. In 1991, for example, a 5,000-year-old mummified corpse was discovered in northern Italy, preserved in the high, cold Alps. With the corpse were two walnut-sized pieces fastened to a leather lace. Scientists determined that the pieces were birch fungus which, when ingested, causes diarrhea, and which is toxic to some bacteria. They also discovered in the corpse's bowels eggs of a parasitic whipworm. From the available evidence, an anthropologist inferred an early-man treatment for a painful bowel condition. How treatments such as this came about is a matter of conjecture, but quite likely they involved much trial, sometimes desperate, and error, sometimes fatal.

Without writing, communication to others about health conditions and treatments would have to rely on folklore and the accumulated knowledge of special family or clan members. Often the cause of an illness was not apparent, and could seem mystical. For a specialist in maladies, the causes and cures thereof, the people might turn to a medicine man or shaman. Uncertainty, doubt, and confusion could be resolved by spiritual recourse, most often with the aid and counsel of a wise person—the medicine man. Such a person could supply the connection between cause and condition, between condition and treatment. The history of medicine is replete with such intermediaries, be they physicians or quacks.

Illness called for a cause or explanation. Repeated experiences, differences and similarities, gave rise to classes of afflictions. Bellyaches, for example, might be classed by location, severity, or duration, and then related to food or drink consumed, or persons or animals contacted. A diagnosis was performed and treatment administered. Over time, the success or failure in treating various classes of bellyaches became an accepted body of knowledge, which, combined with other classes of afflictions, became the institution of medicine.

While knowledge of medicine in pre-historic times must be conjectural, the conjectures are supported or refuted by the study of primitive societies whose present-day lifestyle is believed to be similar to that of ancient people. Aborigines of Australia and New Guinea are studied as stand-ins for their Stone Age ancestors. Native American oral history and traditions help to bridge the gap between written and unwritten history. The painkilling quality of salicylic acid found in willow bark, for example, had been known from ancient times, and then was synthesized into aspirin in the 19th century.

Agriculture enabled, in fact encouraged, human settlement. Human settlements enlarged and with that enlargement came problems of human waste, contagious outbreaks, contaminated water and food, smoke, and collisions. Agriculture enabled populations to grow, and thus enlarged the scope of a health crisis. Power sources that provided warmth and protection also yielded burns and smoke-filled lungs.

Agglomerations of people enabled specialization of manufacturing and services and, in turn, trade and negotiation. Lack of writing impeded, but did not prevent, the transmission and preservation of ideas, including medical experience. Learning in one area may advance the state of knowledge in another area. Insights into human anatomy and maladies, for example, might have arisen from butchering other animals.

For about half of the modern (agriculture) era of humans, medicine developed slowly, each medical crisis dealt with pragmatically. An awareness of invisible forces affecting sickness and health, coupled with a lack of theory or science, allowed the shaman to flourish. Treatments took on a religious quality, and successes or failures were explained without scientific basis. The character of diagnosis evolved with the advance of systematic thought, philosophy, and elemental science, supported by writing, metallurgy, glassmaking, and mummification. Not until the seventh millennium of the modern era, around 500 BC, was serious effort devoted to organizing the thought processes—that is, philosophy. And from there science grew, and medicine benefited.

## Leaving Mystery

The first millennium BC, in which Gore Vidal's historical novel *Creation* is set, was a time of great philosophical awakening. Indeed, the luxury of fiction enabled Vidal to set his creation at exactly December 20, 445 BCE, the beginning date of his narrative response to Herodotus (Vidal, 1981). The perspective of creation here allows no specific dates or moments of "eureka" discovery or invention. During the first millennium BC, however, there were philosophical developments that would have a profound influence on the underpinnings of medicine. The developments reflected increased emphasis on reflective, cogitative, and critical thought to replace instinctive, sensory, or institutional thought. The roots of science and analysis would eventually influence medical diagnosis and treatment. Consider, for example, the complementarity of philosophy and medicine revealed in the works of Empedocles.

Empedocles (495-432 BCE) was a Greek philosopher, physician, physicist, and poet. He is credited with one of the earliest descriptions of the elements of nature—water, air, fire, and earth—which sought to go beyond mystical forces to explain the universe and earthly happenings such as illness. From the idea of elements would one day emerge the periodic table of chemistry and insights into nuclear physics. But Empedocles did not completely abandon his conceptual inheritance. His bridge to earlier mystical forces was achieved with his concepts of Love and Strife, where Love is a force for coming together and Strife for separation or breakup. The interaction of these forces provides for an explanation of life, a cycle of combining and separating. In physiological terms, life emits from the body's internal heat (fire), stabilized or cooled by pneuma or breath (air). From his four elements, the contemporaries and successors of Empedocles described the human condition in terms of a balance of four forces or humors—dry, hot, moist, and cold. Illness was the manifestation of an imbalance in one or more of these forces.

Empedocles' intellectual legacy is contained in fragments of two poems, *Nature* and *Purification*,[60] and some lesser fragments of his work on medicine (Kirk et al., 1983, p. 282). Although he did found a medical school that existed at least to Plato's time, Empedocles' main contribution was to the foundations of scientific thinking. Other pre-Socratics include Democritus, Thales of Miletus, and Heraclitus of Aphesis, each with his own version of the primary force or elements. However, their successor, Hippocrates, is widely regarded as the founding father of medicine.

Hippocrates of Cos (460-380 BCE) was a distinguished physician, author, and collector of leading medical treatises of his time. His name has been given to the oath of medical practice that guides physicians to this day. Although the treatises, whether composed by Hippocrates or others, are now largely obsolete in terms of practice, many of the principles are still relevant. Hippocrates debunked the notion that disease was punishment from the gods, and forwarded external causes of sickness including environmental effects. His method of diagnosis required careful observation and categorization, memory, and reason. His teachings and aphorisms were sufficiently well received as to warrant a school of medical thought. Today he is remembered primarily in terms of his guidelines for medical conduct. The Hippocratic oath provides not only a departure from the mysticism of the past and a reach toward a scientific future, but an ethical foundation for the science and practice of medicine.

For the exciting intellectual era of Hippocrates, Socrates, Plato, and Aristotle, the concept of bodily humors was rather primitive. The humors model required only that the body be a vessel for four ingredients, the proportions of which determined each person's health and well-being. That model was subject to much criticism and many challenging alternatives.

Accounts of Hippocrates' practice and teachings suggest a conservative pragmatism that invoked a sympathetic understanding of nature. The notion of "first, do no harm" seems to inform his diagnoses and treatments. In the creative processes of medicine and medical science, he appeared as a paradigm shift which, at times, could be expressed rather forcefully, as exhibited in his reaction to traditional views of the Sacred Disease" (epilepsy). He writes:

"...with regard to the disease called Sacred: it appears to me to be nowise more divine or more sacred than other diseases, but has a natural cause from which it originates like other affections. Men regard its nature and cause as divine from ignorance and wonder... And this notion of its divinity is kept up by their inability to comprehend it..." (Hippocrates, 1952, p. 154).

The classic period beginning around the time of Plato and Aristotle began to draw concerns about life, health, and mortality into the larger sphere of thought and education.[61] Philosophers were beginning to bridge theory and experience. Aristotle (384-322 BC), son of a physician, furthered the advance of thinking in the foundations of medical science and scientific method. While some of his particulars—e.g., the heart is the seat of senses—were rather off the mark, his overall scheme pointed toward systematic thinking in medicine. In *Motion of Animals*, Aristotle wrote: Elsewhere we have investigated in detail the movement of animals after their various kinds...there remains an investigation of the common ground of any sort of animal movement...we seek general theories...." (Aristotle, p.3)

The Aristotelian tradition was extended by Galen of Pergamum (c.130-219), one of the renowned names at the beginning of a slack period in western medicine. He studied medicine in Alexandria, Egypt, then the leading center of medical knowledge. He returned to Pergamum, Greece, where he gained valuable experience as chief physician to gladiators. He moved to Rome[62] and became a leading figure in medicine and philosophy, based largely on his expositions on anatomy. Galen emphasized the importance of anatomy in the theory and practice of medicine. In addition to some insights he may have gained from the combat injuries of gladiators, he actively dissected and experimented on animals. In his time and long after, dissection of human corpses was forbidden. Nevertheless, he advanced knowledge about the structure and condition of internal organs, though he was sometimes mistaken about their function. He described arteries and blood but was wrong on their relation to human physiology.[63] He noted the ebb and flow of blood in arteries, but did not understand blood circulation.

Galen carried over many conceptions from Hippocrates, including the conveniently general "humors," derived from the four elements and primary qualities hot, cold, wet, and dry. These qualities were applied to particular organs as well as to the whole physique, thus further emphasizing the importance of anatomy in medical science. Galen was a philosopher with a wide range of interests, and a prolific author on a variety of subjects, including medical science. His influence on medicine lasted well into the next millennium.[64]

The fall of the Roman Empire took with it any significant progress in medicine. The rise of Christianity, with its various superstitions, contributed to prohibitions about human anatomical inquiry.

Alchemy in pursuit of the magic formula for converting base metal into gold gave impetus to chemistry. In the wonderful process of creation, faulty premises sometimes can lead to destructive or useful conclusions. Medical science is replete with well-intended cures such as venesection (phlebotomy or bloodletting) grounded in a naive theory that produced toxic events. On the other hand, mistakes and accidents were sometimes serendipitous; leftover mold in a petri dish, for example, signaled penicillin.

## Anatomy

Successful intervention of humans in the state of their health implies, above all, a knowledge about the object of their concern—their physique, their body, and all its parts and connections. But that knowledge suffered a prolonged introduction, slowed in no small measure by mystical musings, faulty assumptions, and religious or social restraints. Galen's authoritative writings, based heavily on dissection of non-human animals, led to some errors long accepted in medical science. While progress in anatomy was stunted in western Europe for nearly a millennium after Galen, it continued apace in the Arabic world.

While western Europe was in political and social disarray, Islamic scholars contributed much to preservation and advances in medicine. The vast texts from Hellenistic and Roman times were translated into Arabic, and from these translations arose questions about and corrections to the original. The enduring works of Galen were carefully studied, translated, and extended by Rhazes, a renowned court physician in Baghdad who made major contributions to neuroanatomy. At the end of the 10th century, advances in neurology were made by the Persian physician, Avicennia, who also produced a primary textbook on medicine used in Europe well into the 18th century. His contemporary in Moorish Spain, Al-Zahrawi, wrote more than 30 books on medicine, including extensive contributions to brain and spine surgery.

The Islamic scholars accounted for much of the development in medicine until the Enlightenment in western Europe arose to overcome the stultifying influence of the church. Between about 1489 and 1515, an awakening in western science of anatomy appeared in the detailed drawings of human parts by Leonardo da Vinci. He based his detailed illustrations on dissections of 30 corpses, until he was ordered to stop by Pope Leo X. That was just two years before Martin Luther began a distraction that probably had a strong influence on the free thinking needed for support of science.

In 1543, the Flemish physician, Andreas Vesalius, wrote *Fabrica*, "...a publication so scientific that it initiated medical science itself." (Friedman and Friedland, 1998, p. 14). From Vesalius, his students, and his successors came major advances in anatomy and medical science still underway today. His studies of the nervous system broke with Aristotelian tradition by connecting nerves to the brain rather than heart. He further demonstrated that nerves were not hollow tubes.

By Renaissance times, European anatomists understood, and had exposed, much about the human physique. Bones and sinews were pictured, organs were described, arteries and veins were revealed, and blood accounted for, if not always correctly. Some of these revelations resulted in the authors being burned at the stake.

This understanding of the body's structural components yielded knowledge of its connective matter, like blood and nerves. William Harvey is credited with the discovery of the circulatory system in 1616, but his findings benefited by the works of others in the 16ᵗʰ century. Harvey explained the role of heart, blood, and the mechanics of its circulation.

Awareness of the nervous system goes back to Hippocrates and earlier, but major advances awaited Peyligk on brain parts at the end of the 15ᵗʰ century and Vesalius for his mid-16ᵗʰ century work on cranial nerves, meninges, spinal and peripheral nerves, and the brain's vascular components. High-powered microscopes capable of examining cells were needed to understand transmission of electrical signals between neurons, and this occurred in the mid-19ᵗʰ and 20ᵗʰ centuries. Modern science continues its task of solving neurological mysteries such as Alzheimer's disease.[65]

## Afflictions

As humans evolve, so do their afflictions, and their cures. Some diseases achieve such a massive scale that they threaten the survival of many if not all humans. Some persist as a chronic erosion of human health and viability. Some recede, or seem conquered, then reappear. A few examples are plague, smallpox, flu, malaria, cholera, tuberculosis, polio, yellow fever, and war. The story of mankind is also a story of diseases and remedies. An old Arab aphorism holds that God creates cures to all afflictions, save one—old age. The latter will not be addressed here. Instead a few examples will reveal the challenges, human responses, and outcomes—as of now.

Plague, in its generic sense, covers a wide variety of conditions, all bad for people. It might include a "plague of locusts," for example, or just a widespread disease or condition. However, *the* Plague or Black Death of Europe in the 14th century, and other outbreaks in earlier times, was a particularly vicious killer. It is called bubonic plague from the formation of buboes, large painful growths in the armpit and groin that burst and secrete pus. The cure rate with some antibiotics can be as high as 75 percent if treatment is timely. In its septicemic form, it enters the bloodstream and is not detectable until just prior to death. In pneumonic form it enters the lungs, causing sudden death.

Although Plague is known to have occurred at least as far back as the 6th century, its most notorious incidence was in 1347-48, when it killed over 60 percent of Europe's population. The Plague terrified people who had no idea of its cause, a flea-carried bacterium that infects rodents which then spread the diseased fleas to the human population. When the epidemic struck, people panicked, fled, and blamed their fate on the sins of the community or on some scapegoat. The germ theory was yet unknown.

Cases of Plague still appear in small numbers in Madagascar, Tanzania, Brazil, Peru, Burma, and Viet Nam. Parts of Africa and China appear to be a permanent source of the disease. In the U.S., about a dozen cases are reported per year, mainly in western States.[66] Caught in time, bubonic plague is treatable with some antibiotics such as streptomycin, but not with the time-honored penicillin. Of special concern is the report of an antibiotic-resistant form of the Plague bacterium. This will require that humans' protective science again evolve to meet the challenge.

Smallpox is a virus with a long history, with evidence of outbreaks in northeastern Africa 12,000 years ago. Its presence is detectable in Egyptian mummies from more than 3,000 years ago. Smallpox played a significant role in the European invasion and conquest of the Americas. Following Cortez's invasion of America in the 16th century, more than 18 million Amerindians died from the disease, some of it intentionally spread as a weapon of occupation.

Discovery of susceptibility and resistance to the disease was a fortuitous quirk of nature and medical theory/testing. First efforts at immunization began by observing that persons who got smallpox and survived were immune from re-infection. So, about 1,000 years ago, a tentative practice was to infect patients with small amounts of smallpox scabs in the hope that it would cause a mild, recoverable case of smallpox. The strategy produced mixed results. Then, late in the 18th century, Edward Jenner noticed that milkmaids who recovered from the mild disease cowpox seemed immune from smallpox. Jenner, ignoring Hippocratic restraints, vaccinated[67] a young boy with cowpox pus, then smallpox. Jenner's theory held, the boy survived, and Jenner is now credited with establishing vaccination as a tool in preventive medicine.

Officially, smallpox has been eliminated except for laboratory stocks in Russia and the United States. However, it remains a biohazard and potential weapon of bioterrorism.

Malaria is caused by neither bacterium nor virus but by protozoan parasites injected into the victim's bloodstream by the anopheles mosquito. Symptoms include fever, intense chills, diarrhea, vomiting, pain, and death. Although there are meliorating drugs and preventive measures, there is as yet no vaccine and it continues its killing ways, particularly in Sub-Saharan Africa.

The medical history of malaria exemplifies the cumulative process of knowledge creation. Malaria gets its name from "mal" (bad) and "aria" (air) because of the ancient belief that the malady was rooted in noxious vapors arising from stagnant water or swamps. Records as old as writing itself describe the symptoms of this swamp fever, often referring to evil gods, particular seasons, swampy conditions, and even linking the fever to the presence of mosquitoes. Scientists in the late 18th century began to doubt the "bad air" theory. The Italian Lancisi in 1717 considered the possibility of mosquitoes injecting something into the victim's blood. John Crawford in 1796 vanquished the vapors idea in favor of mosquitoes as the cause of malaria. Josiah Nott in 1850 noted microscopic abnormalities in the blood of malarial victims. Charles Leveran in 1880 observed the movement of a parasite in blood. Soon thereafter Louis Pasteur and others confirmed Leveran's findings. Ronald Ross in 1898 identified the anopheles mosquito as the malarial vector. Research was enhanced by technology in imaging, biology, chemistry, and engineering. By 2002, the genome of mosquito and parasite had been sequenced.

Meantime, the plasmodium parasite evolved and became resistant to drugs used to reduce malaria's effects. And the struggle against malaria's parasite, vector, and habitat goes on.

Other diseases impact the human body and mind in ways ranging from discomfort to swift, certain death. Many maladies have long, lingering, disabling effects requiring protracted care and expensive treatments.[68] Some, like tuberculosis and flu, evolve into new forms that must be combated with new treatments. Some, like malaria and HIV/AIDS, are treatable but, as yet, incurable. Laboratories and scientists are immersed in preventing and controlling epidemics.

Occupational and athletic rigors expose human anatomical limitations and fragilities, some of which result from changes in environment and activity. Evolution is a slow process, and human anatomy cannot always remodel itself to accommodate the pace of new needs and strains. Stress fractures of bones and sprains of ligaments are common in some athletics. Strength advantages in some sports have prompted the abuse of performance-enhancing drugs like metabolic steroids. Occupations such as coal mining have increased the incidence of lung damage. Specialties such as sports medicine have developed to deal with problems common to athletes.

Behaviorally oriented conditions—such as lung cancer from smoking, AIDS from unprotected sexual activity or injections with infected needles, and diabetes from poor eating habits—extend the realm of medicine beyond the laboratory. Controlling vectors such as rodents and insects are important interventions in disease control. Regulation and inspection may help to eliminate toxic substances from food, drink, and air. Recognizing and treating the conditions of persons deficient in self-discipline may be equally as important as a pill protocol. Improved information systems can help physicians to identify symptoms and design treatments.

Mechanics of human repair and supplementation include mediation of trauma impacts (blood transfusion), restoration of damaged body parts (setting a bone), adding capacity (eyeglasses and hearing aids), making up a deficiency (pacemaker), and replacing missing or inoperative parts (prostheses, joint replacement). All these masterworks of human engineering enable the human animal to survive longer and  to be functionally useful in that longer life. Whether this longevity is preferable, for the long-run survival and development of the species, to a more rapid turnover in humans is more a philosophical than medical concern.

War may be considered by some as beyond the realm of medicine or medical intervention. But it is a social disease that so ravages the human condition that it should not be ignored, and perhaps it is not beyond the models of human medical science and engineering.[69] War's symptoms are akin to cancer's. Rogue cells attack the host, and a struggle for territory and well-being ensues. The tumor is removed, destroyed, or contained and the patient is treated, or it metastasizes and consumes the victim. Were it not for the human devastation caused by war, its qualities as a disease could be taken as a simple metaphor. In fact, war has caused, and continues to cause, human damage at such an enormous scale in medical terms that it cannot be ignored. In addition to death and disabilities, resources that might be devoted to science and curing are squandered in destruction.

## Pathogens and Knowledge

Germ theory, with inklings in the first century BC and earlier, was furthered in the 1670s by Antony Leeuwenhoek and later by others. Credit for the clear statement and verification of the germ theory is often given to Louis Pasteur, who in the 1860s confirmed disease caused by living, reproducing organisms, and showed how disease was communicated by unhygienic practices.

Confirmation of germ theory was a monumental achievement of medical science. Relieved of mysticism, religion, and paranormal beliefs,[70] investigators could develop new theories and tests for disease detection and analysis. Germ theory also represents the creative process of collaboration, criticism, and consensus required for successful diagnosis and cure of ailments.

The microscope developed by Leeuwenhoek began the evolution of ever-more powerful tools of information about the minute structures of the human body and the sources of its maladies. The X-ray was developed at the end of the 19th century by Wilhelm Rontgen and others, followed in the 20th century by magnetic resonance imaging, computed tomography scanning, and ultrasound machines. These devices—with other measuring and internal scanning probes, all tied to computers—have expanded the capacity of medicine to harness information for medical research and diagnoses. DNA was successfully modeled by James Watson and Francis Crick in 1953, basing their work on that of Rosalind Franklin and Maurice Wilkins and a series of scientists tracing back to the pioneering genetic research of Gregor Mendel. The DNA model explained the internal information process by which characteristics are passed on, generation by generation, in an evolving species. DNA, deoxyribonucleic acid, is the material from which messages are made to tell the cells how to form and what to do. From four basic letters, ATGC, biological words are formed, arranged into chromosomal sentences, and sequenced into instructions for building and operating a living organism. DNA, chemically, is phosphate, sugar, and the four nitrogen bases A(adenine), T(thymine), G(guanine), and C(cytosine), known long before the actual structure of the DNA molecule was discovered. The double helix structure, revealed by Watson and Crick, became the architectural language of biological science by showing how cells were constructed and how they replicate. As letters become words and sentences in a literary message by their sequence, ATGCs become genome messages by their sequences. Deciphering the DNA was actively pursued in the 1960s and the human genome was completely sequenced, or fully written, in 2000. It represented a milestone achievement in science, with great potential for analyzing and diagnosing human defects and diseases and for developing new cures.

As knowledge of anatomy expanded physician's options for mending and dosing patients to health, so the understanding of genetic material and structure has produced a new outlook for plant and animal engineering. DNA is the underpinning of that new outlook. Genetic modification already has had a substantial impact on the design of plants and some animals. Synthetic biology may soon produce stocks of standard biological parts, available to scientists and biological engineers for building or repairing living things. The technical possibilities for altering life forms are so formidable that it warrants extensive public scrutiny.

Consider, for example, the redesign of the human form to better accommodate the projected environment on earth. That redesign might include making people smarter, stronger, and smaller. *Smarter* to assume the takeover of nature's responsibility of controlling survival and limiting growth of the species; *stronger* to withstand the impacts of disease and a toxic environment; *smaller* to survive and prosper with less pressure on the planet's limited resources.[71] The potential impact of genetic management warrants serious thought, from physicians to philosophers and politicians.

## Contraception

Nature bestowed on humans a generous procreative capacity. Before agriculture, that capacity offset the equally generous mortality of the species. As hunter-gatherers, our limited numbers did not overburden natural resources. If a source of sustenance did give out, the tribe moved on. Being omnivorous and inventive helped. A mobile lifestyle permitted access to new sources of food, shelter, and materials, but also sidestepped the contagions of large settlements. The hunter-gatherers may have faced a life that was "...poore, nasty, brutish, and short" (Hobbes, 1950, p. 104), but abundant reproduction offset the high mortality rates and short life expectancy. Perhaps most important for the species' survival, the hunter-gatherers were clustered in small numbers, widely separated, so that obliterating tragedies were attenuated.

Agriculture enabled humans to eat better and regularly and devote only part of their energy and attention to providing food. Some people were freed up to make tools, better homes, and items of trade. Settlements grew. So did trash, dirt, and disease. Closeness caused contagions, some so devastating that whole populations were wiped out. Some scholars suggest that life expectancy of modern populations were, at times, less than that of the hunter-gatherers.[72] Until relatively recently, nature took dramatic tolls on the human population, but in the past millennium or so, medicine has intervened in illness and death. Medicine has lowered the death rate of babies and baby-bearers. Medicine has postponed the death of the sick and injured. Even war injuries produce fewer deaths in relation to disabilities. Medicine has extended the life of the aged. All told, agriculture, energy, and medicine, aided by the principle of the exponential, have enabled a very recent, rapid rise in the human population. One limiting factor is birth control, exercised by mating couples. Although methods for human intervention in reproduction are a distinct specialization in medicine, many aspects of medical research, education, and practice touch on reproduction. Chemical (spermicide), hormonal (pill), barrier (diaphragm, condom) and surgical (vasectomy, tubectomy) methods all provide protection against pregnancy with little, or no, change in sexual behavior. So why are human populations expanding so rapidly?

Intentions to limit pregnancy and/or birth have a long history. Reliable contraception is considerably more recent. The ancient Egyptian text, *Papyrus Ebers,* contained "recipes" for abortifacients (Jutte, 2008, p. 29). Christian, Judaic, and Muslim scripture is replete with references to, and judgments on, procreation and its avoidance. Much of the history of contraception contains references to myths and weird, even comical, practices. The condom has a long history, but became a really effective, inexpensive barrier method only after Goodyear's development of the vulcanization process in the early 19$^{th}$ century and product refinements in the 20$^{th}$ century. Hormonal preventive birth controls came into use in the early 1960s, followed by the emergency contraceptive pill. Methods for preventing pregnancy are widely variable and available so that family planning is practical. But the step from individual control of pregnancy to planetary population control is huge. Policies and programs to limit population size must connect individual and collective behavior.

It is not surprising that individuals, families, firms, and clans seeking their immediate welfare behave in ways inconsistent with the well-being of a larger community or nation. In older agricultural societies, for example, large families provided a cheap, abundant supply of farm labor. Also in such societies, children were a source of old-age security. In more recent times, parenthood may lead to children and/or parents becoming a family or social burden. In part because they were initiated too late, the "one child only" policies in China, and the compulsory sterilization policies in India, have been unnecessarily harsh, yet inadequate, in limiting the large populations in those two countries.

Are there ways of relating individual incentives to larger community goals? Yes. Consider emulating, for example, the "cap and trade" mechanism used in air pollution management. After determining the nation's desired population or growth rate, fertility options would be made available, perhaps adjusted to age cohorts. The options would be tradeable. Persons preferring to sell their fertility "credit" to persons seeking one would establish the value and market.

## Body's Life: Span and Quality

The creation of medicine, like the creation of agriculture and fire management, is a series of stages built on knowledge and experience, the back-and-forth of thinking and doing. A clear notion of the body's inner workings and arrangement awaited human dissection and anatomy. The confirmation of microscopically small building units of cells and germs awaited the microscope's evidence. The theory of generational inheritance of traits or characteristics was bolstered by Gregor Mendel's proofs in a pea pod. The concept of the double helix to store and transfer information was validated with genome sequencing. Genetic management is leaving nature's random world of trait succession by Darwinian selection, and entering mankind's designer world of synthetic biology.[73]

The 21st century began with tangible progress in "regenerative medicine," that is, reconstruction of body parts from a patient's own cells. A failing kidney, for example, can be replaced with a new one grown from the patient's harvested cells and molded to comply with the patient's particular requirements. No wait for donor supply. No fear of organ rejection. Regenerative medicine holds promise for tissue reconstruction after trauma or correction of chronic disabilities. It is another aspect of the ultimate intervention of humans into the afflictions arising from the workings of nature, and other humans.

Ever present in medicine, as in the other avenues of human creation, are the mysteries and uncertainties attending each addition to knowledge.

The good news about medicine's successful intervention on behalf of *Homo sapien* health is that it protected the expansion of the species number to 7 billion.

The bad news is that, by thwarting nature's pathogens from doing their unkind business, earth now has 7 billion crowded, mobile people. Pandemic arrest requires enormous medical intervention. The natural quarantine of widely spaced people is no longer a public health asset. Minor health problems become major health problems simply as a matter of scale. And the success of medicine's creation places increased burden on human's other creations, agriculture and energy. The survival, well-being, and lifespan of an ever growing population will depend less on nature's ways and more on human creativity and intervention.

# Money

Three creations of humans—agriculture, fire control, and medicine—are, at root, relations of man to nature; more precisely, they represent human interventions in nature's processes of species selection, sustenance, and modification.[74] As populations grew and became more interdependent, reflective, and sophisticated, humans turned their creativity to the relations among themselves. Three creations serving as organizing forces among humans are money, logic, and writing.

First, consider money, a bonding element of trade, production, and saving.

## Medium of Exchange: The First Derivative

"Money is a social relation. Like the meaning of a word, or the proper form of a ritual, it exists as part of a system of behavior shared by a group of people." (Foley, 1987)[75]

The roots of money are in trade, exchange. A shepherd offering a goat for a measure of a farmer's grain signaled specialization in herding and cultivation. That specialization brought about efficiencies. Overall, trade produced more goats and more grain than if each agriculturist raised his own goats and grew his own grain.

Basic economics in a simple society states that if goats grow scarce relative to grain, a trade will require more grain to obtain a goat.[76] As long as trades were local, tradable goods and traders were few. Individual exchanges, or barter, were adequate. As populations grew, as goods became diversified and abundant, and as traders grew more distant and unfamiliar, the need for an expression of value, or medium of exchange, became necessary. A successful system of trade and exchange rests on reliable expectations, or trust. Even the most elemental barter transactions rely on standards of quality (say, of goats and grain).[77] And contracts for future delivery depend upon the consistency of the measures, as well as the reliability of the deliverer. When barter was local, simple, and among persons well-known to each other, mechanisms for enforcement were seldom needed. As transactions became more elaborate— involving unacquainted/third parties or consummated over long time spans—enforcers and/or insurers were needed.

A goat doesn't fit in a pocket, nor does it store conveniently. Grain stores but can be bulky. So representations of valued objects such as goats and grains came into use well into the agricultural-settlement era. The shekel, for example, began as a token for a weight in grain, then for a weight in precious metal. Media of exchange such as cattle, beaver pelts, shells, grain, and gold possessed some intrinsic value. Metals such as copper and bronze had some intrinsic value, but also took on representational value. Coins came to reflect less their metallic value and more what the coin came—by custom, law, and trade— to represent. Institutions were developed to enforce the regularity of value. The value of coinage was derived from its economy.

From trade and exchange sprang the creative abstraction of money. Just as the creation of agriculture emerged from hunting and gathering, the creation of money emerged from barter trading. Creating money evolved to building economies—complex and, at times, mysterious processes. Consider a first step, coinage.

## Coinage

Modern economy began with the emergence of an abstract expression of value, money, roughly 5 millennia ago, midway between the beginnings of modern humans and the present. The transition from straight barter was achieved by using a bartered object, such as a measure of grain, to serve as a medium of exchange, a sort of currency. Money arose when the widely accepted unit of value was represented by a token. For example, a Sumerian word for wheat, she, combined with a bushel measure, kel, became shekel, and the shekel was coined as a basic monetary unit.[78] The transition was consummated when metallic coins, whose intrinsic or use value was a fraction of the value they represented, became widely used and frequently exchanged. Money became the first derivative of trade and exchange. Its evolution continues.

Coin is both noun and verb. To "coin a phrase," for example, is to create or establish an addition to language. Origins of coin as a word include the Middle English "coigne," the Middle French "coin," and Latin "cuneus," for wedge or die. Coins are created by pressing or striking images on the metal blank. Over time, coinage processes standardized the metal content and enhanced designs to deter counterfeiting or shaving. Metal coins were/are durable, portable, and convenient. They have been formed in a variety of shapes, sizes, and denominations. In time, other representations of value—on paper with a declared printed value and encryptions to deter counterfeiting—supplemented or replaced coins. More recently, money takes the form of an electronic accounting entry.

The most critical ingredient in any currency—whether coin, paper, or plastic—is trust, the assurance that it is redeemable in the value it represents. That trust rests on the capacity of someone or some entity to assure a currency's value. Such capacity became the responsibility of government, often asserted by stamping a leader's likeness on the coin, printing its declaration on the paper, or specifying its assurances in a contract.

## Banks: The Second Derivative

It was, indeed, a marvelous invention whereby all items of commerce could be represented in a common metric, money, which could be stored for future transactions. However, as the use of money became more common, so did its forms, sizes, and the values represented. The variation became vexing. For example, in the Judaic temples offerings could be made only in one denomination, the half-shekel. Moneychangers were available to facilitate the tribute, notoriously shaving a few points on each exchange of currency.

Moneychangers evolved into "banks" when their clients had some surplus in need of safe storage for later withdrawal. Banks accepted currency and issued a receipt, something like a certificate of deposit. When the procedure became routine, receipts were drawn simply to bearer, enabling the clients to use the certificates in their own trades. The certificates were traded again and again without going to the bank for a withdrawal of the original money. Noting the infrequency of actual withdrawal, banks profitably issued more certificates than could be supported by the reserves created by deposits. Banks came to expect that not everybody would seek withdrawal at the same time, an act of faith in the mechanics of the system. So banks made money.

As the money system expanded, so did the opportunities to gain from risky, even fraudulent, practices. Governments began to intervene through a monopoly on the issuance of coins and other forms of money, and by regulating fiduciary practices such as reserve requirements. The world of money had taken on a reality of its own, beyond merely representing the value of goods and services. Money begat its own markets, its own suppliers, its own traders, its own regulators. And as the goat-trader took the coin as a promise of value for, say, a measure of grain, so money traders and managers used money promises as their stock in trade.

Banks and banking evolved as the corpus of the money concept. Some contend that banks actually preceded money, but banks as we know them arose in Europe in the 13<sup>th</sup> and 14<sup>th</sup> centuries.[79] The term "bank" derives from the Italian *banca*, reflecting banking's significance in Venice and Florence where the Medici clan held sway. Most of the basic elements of modern banking were in place by the end of the 17<sup>th</sup> century. Of the three functions of money—medium of exchange, store of value, unit of account—the evolution of moneychanging into banking was predicated on the latter two. A twist on the store of value came in the form of lending, where a promise of future repayment is exchanged for current money as cash or entry in account. Despite vast differences in scale, forms, terms, and mechanics, banking consists simply of holding or lending money—often above the bank's reserves.

## The Money Industry: Promises, Promises

The money industry parallels other industries that actually make things or perform tangible services. Notwithstanding interaction with these other industries, the money industry makes trades and enters into contracts that have little or nothing to do with inventing, building, repairing, storing, and transporting stuff, or performing services. The values of all these goods and services are mirrored in money. And some of them are promissory money, or credit.

A common element of this money world is trust–allied with reliability, confidence, assurance, and, in the event of failure, remedy. That remedy, broadly defined, is insurance. For example, Americans who deposit funds in a bank have the backing of the Federal Deposit Insurance Corporation. Even if the bank fails completely, depositors, within limits, have their funds protected.

Other assurances of the orderly operation of the banking system have been developed by institutions centrally operated or overseen by national governments. In America that institution is the Federal Reserve System, as championed in principle by Alexander Hamilton and others who argued for the establishment of a single central bank (ultimately the First and Second National Banks). President Andrew Jackson and others passionately opposed the idea of a central national bank. Banking, as with many institutions in America, has wavered between central and state authority, and between governmental regulation and private control. While the Federal Government now has a monopoly on the manufacture of currency,[80] including protection against counterfeits, the supply of money is managed by a complex of institutions with the Federal Reserve Bank at its heart.

The Federal Reserve System is of relatively recent origin. The Federal Reserve Act was passed in 1913, following extensive study of the rigidities in money supply and bank reserve requirements. Rather than one central bank, a political compromise created a system of 12 regional banks and 25 branch banks that serve federally chartered (national) and some state-chartered banks. The regional banks conduct the business of the Federal Reserve System and participate in the decisionmaking of the central Fed in Washington, DC. The Federal Reserve Bank is managed by a seven-member Board of Governors, appointed in rotation by U.S. Presidents. All functions of the Fed are subject to oversight by the U.S. Congress. The Fed regulates the supply of money in three ways: buying and selling Federal government securities, establishing the interest (discount) rate on short-term loans between banks, and setting the reserve requirements of banks. Although the Fed is a powerful influence on the Nation's money supply, recent experience has revealed that other entities and devices, outside of the Fed's authority, can greatly influence the management of money and, accordingly, the condition of the Nation's economy.

Operations of the Federal Open Market Committee are a key factor in the supply of the Nation's money. FOMC operations embody the banking idea. The FOMC—consisting of the Federal Reserve's Board of Governors and five of the regional bank presidents—conducts all open-market operations through the Reserve

Bank of New York, constituting a complete monopoly. The FOMC increases the supply of money by buying government securities[81] from banks with money, which can then be used for lending. Conversely, selling securities soaks up bank funds, thus reducing funds available for lending. The actual effect, of course, depends on a variety of forces deeply imbedded in the national psyche.[82] The essence of banking is making money. And ever since moneylenders squatted in the temple, money has been made on trust, namely that funds given over to the fiduciary would be available when requested, and that money reserves are sufficient to withstand withdrawal demands. "Reserve" is the most basic banking illusion, a fancy, institutionalized term for lying about money. It underlies the way the FOMC is able to increase or decrease the money supply[83] and influence the inflationary or deflationary trend of the economy.

## Other Derivatives

The backup insurance of bank accounts provided by the FDIC and the trading and regulating operations of the FOMC are powerful tools in the control of the Nation's money supply. However, there are financial devices outside of FDIC and FOMC authority or watch that influence the monetary condition of the Nation. For example, devices that grew out of the risk-distributing features of market hedging have been used for market gambling. However, when the market sours, these devices can result in losses completely beyond the capacity of insuring funds to cover. A substantial share of credit derivatives operate outside of current Federal regulation. Credit default swaps, for example, enable buyers and sellers to trade on the uncertainty surrounding the solvency of a business. In other words, for a fee, an insurer (or reinsurer) assumes the risk of the financial consequences from a business failure. There is a risk that the insurer will write more of such contracts than can be honored if, say, many businesses fail altogether. Then the insurers of the insurers absorb the losses, and if too many insurers fail at the same time, the re-insurers fail, and so on. When players in the money lending or money derivatives game sense that the probabilities of default are increasing, they will increase fees, tighten the terms of contracts, or withdraw—all actions that restrict money flow and, if strong enough, depress the real economy.

At the root of money derivatives is promise, trust, faith. The faith-based institution of money lending or banking rests on the idea of <u>reserve</u>, a supply of funds known to be inadequate to cover all potential withdrawals by depositors. The very basis of the modern economy—money—relies on the power of myth. But then, the economy is but one dimension of an organized society that incorporates many other myths and mysteries.

## Money and Economy

Can an economy exist without money? Certainly. Economies exist when there are limited resources and capabilities to make or acquire desired things–goods, services, experiences. Economic decisions arise about how to get the most things at the least cost, or how best to spend one's time and where. Economics includes learning the fastest, easiest, and cheapest way to perform a task; deciding whether to consume or save; and deciding whether to make an object yourself or make something else and trade. Trade and economy is possible without money. Barter economies work, but without the lubricant of money, trade and the economies on which trade depends are limited.

The conventional definition says money is a medium of exchange, store of value. To these two functions might be added a unit of account.[84] A medium of exchange must have widespread acceptance, a convenient metric, and ease of handling and counting. A store of value implies a reliable rate of exchange in the future. A unit of account implies an established institution facile and reliable in records of account.

Inherent in a money system is a body of promises, promises by authority on the reliability of money. Users of money rely on the authenticity and adequacy of money, the capacity of the system to prevent counterfeiting, forgery, or the unauthorized emptying of accounts. The monetary system is a system of promises among authorities, managers, insurers, and users. Success of the system and the economy on which it depends hinges on reliability and trust.

The discipline of economics separates itself into micro economy and macro economy, the former focused on the individual decisions of persons and firms about maximizing profitability, minimizing costs, and consuming to most satisfaction. In the micro economy, money is a convenient measure of value when making decisions about, or evaluating the success of, a combination of resources in production, a selection of enterprises, a basket of consumer items, or the makeup of an investment portfolio. Micro choices may be made for oneself, for one's firm, or as a fiduciary on behalf of another.

Macro economy is concerned with the collective performance of a unit, such as a nation, in terms of aggregate production, employment, growth, price levels, and so on. Gross Domestic Product, for example, is a size measure, expressed in money, of all the output of goods and services, commonly of a nation, for a period of time. The importance of money in the macro economy is so significant that, in a sense, money defines the macro economy. Indeed, one school of macroeconomics, the monetarists, treats economic policy largely as the management of the money supply. The money supply determines the "price" of money in relation to all goods and services.

Why is the price of money important? After all, money is just a proxy so its relative amount shouldn't matter. The problem is cheap money (inflation) or expensive money (deflation) does not affect all money users equally. And, critically, changes in the price of money (hence, prices of everything else) affect expectations and behavior. For example, inflation might encourage some producers to enlarge inventories in the belief that inflation will increase their value. Or, amid deflation, individuals and organizations will save money on the belief that it will buy more in the future. Some money savings are achieved by reducing production and increasing unemployment.

The role of money in the modern economy may be likened to that of blood circulation in anatomy. Blood does not independently perform body activity. Rather, blood's function is to carry life-sustaining ingredients throughout the body and to sweep up the body's crud to be reprocessed or eliminated. Money's value is nil except in circulative service to producers, consumers, lenders, and borrowers. Money's regulators, to the extent they serve the corpus of economy and not money handlers, seek to manage the rate of money flow between the highs of inflation and the lows of depression.

## Creative Destruction

The life and death of firms and enterprises in a thriving, active economy is captured in Joseph Schumpeter's *creative destruction*.[85] This concept refers to the death of a process, firm, or institution to make way for a new way of doing things. Usually, creative destruction is driven by innovation or a set of innovations. Innovation, almost by definition, implies abandonment of existing ways of doing things. And that giving up of old ways is fraught with uncertainty. Not just monetary establishments but whole industries or economies resist uncertainty even when the prospects of change in the long run are positive. The resistance is more entrenched when the longrun benefits are to the larger economy or industry at the expense and/or collapse of individual firms. After all, the business of business is profitability, and uncertainty and risks—including those of innovation—are costs to be avoided. Businesses are not public service entities. The strategy of individual firms is to avoid such costs by sitting tight or shifting costs to some other entity such as government.

Uncertainty deters adoption of a procedure or technology whose effect has not been confirmed by experience—the essence of conservatism. A manufacturer would prefer to follow an old labor-intensive process rather than a new labor-saving, capital-intensive process, *if* cheap labor can be accessed. Nothing stirs the entrepreneur's interest in invention and adoption of innovations more than expensive labor. Mechanized cotton pickers and combines would not have been adopted if farmers were not threatened with rising labor costs. So when farm labor drifted to better paying jobs in the city, it became more expensive to harvest cotton and grain. But the rates of historical versus projected costs and returns were uncertain. Hence, the rate of adopting the machine technologies depended upon the entrepreneur's ability to reduce or shift uncertainty. The potential advantage of an innovation to the public at large is likely to be greater than to the individual firms at any given point of time, if for no other reason than uncertainty. This uncertainty argues for a public or community investment in innovations and the creativity that produces them.

## Scale

During the period of extreme economic distress beginning in 2008, some policy measures were powered by a fear that some financial organizations were "too big to fail." Over a period of expansion, acquisition, and mergers, some banks, insurers, and other financial institutions had grown so large that insolvency would have widespread impacts. The deficiencies in the financial sector spilled over into the productive sectors of the economy; consumers, producers, and financiers grew too fearful to act, and recession resulted. From this experience, a lesson to be learned about economy, and perhaps social organization generally, is that if an organization is too big to fail, it probably should be divided or recomposed.

Drawing on the metaphor of nature, we note that colonies of life forms outgrow their ability to sustain themselves (say, by destruction of food supply, epidemic, internal conflict, predator growth, etc.). Error or mishap in the colony leaves no restorative remnants, so it is completely wiped out. So might it go with an entire species.

Death is an important part of life, not just of individuals but of clans, societies, and their organizations. Humans were designed to live within nature's means, with fertility, activity, and mortality levels to sustain the population. Intervention in nature comes at some risk, and the same wisdom applied to agriculture, energy, or health must be applied to creations such as money. Firms, like populations, can be too large. Small isn't just beautiful,[86] it is practical and useful.

## Money's Role

Money is the organizing instrument of economy. For that reason alone, money can claim the scale, diversity, and accomplishments of modern society. Without money, trade would be limited to local personal transactions. Money in its many forms—coin, paper, plastic, and electronic blip—provides a widely accepted index of value and exchange. Lending money bridges current economic activity and future repayment.

Money in its many variants and involvements is a vital feature of society, yet it remains an abstraction.[87] The usefulness of money depends on the economy, another abstraction describing people's production, trade, and consumption of goods and services. Money institutions, many outside of traditional banks, are complex, opaque, and self-serving.[88] The myths and mysteries of money and economy remain, some intentionally.

The good news about money is that it has facilitated the production of ever more things and services to serve ever more people. The bad news is that money and its control has inequitably distributed the benefits of that enlarged productive capacity. The money system has served wealth, not necessarily economic justice.

# Logic

"Aristotle's creation of this new discipline of thought, and his firm establishment of its essential lines, remain among the lasting achievements of the human mind." Durant[89]

Reasoning—in the sense of assembling, arranging, and analyzing information for a useful conclusion—transcends the whole of human existence.[90] The creation of logic, however, should be assigned a later point in the evolution of thought. That point is not when humans began thinking, but when they began thinking about thinking.

Logic is about orderly relations between and among statements. The essence of those orderly relations applied to persons, species, clans, and nations is the contribution of logic to society. Thinking about thinking is tool building. The tools are reason and its descendents—science, governance, technology, community, and vision—vital to humans who have come so completely to rely on reason for participation and survival. In support of logic, thinking about thinking perhaps could be extended somewhat. A broader view might include, say, the forms of knowledge (epistemology), the nature of existence and causes (metaphysics), the guides of behavior (ethics), and many other components of what is grouped under, and labeled, philosophy. For now, though, the narrower view will do.

The creative element in thinking about thinking is the design for critical evaluation—detection for correction. Criticism, with defense or acceptance, is at the heart of modern human evolution, perhaps survival. Reasoned critique is a powerful organizing force in a successful, healthy, society.

## Origins

As with other human creations, logic did not appear at a single time and place, but rested on earlier events and contemplations, and developed over time, via criticism. King and Shapiro open their compressed history of logic[91] with the assertion: "Aristotle was the first thinker to devise a logical system." But they immediately follow that statement with credits to Socrates, Zeno of Elea, Parmenides, Plato, and others for building materials of *Organon*, the Aristotelian system. As a reference point for the development of logic in Western philosophy, Aristotle still appears to be the prominent candidate. His syllogisms dominate the history of rules for valid argument.

The syllogism, root of Aristotelian logic, is a form of argument designed to produce valid conclusions. Validity of argument is concerned with consistency in the reasoning process, not necessarily the "reality" of the outcome. Truth, in the sense of reality, depends on the accuracy or correctness of the premises. Perfectly valid arguments do not necessarily lead to truthful/reality conclusions. Nevertheless, to be valid, arguments must be logically constructed. Commonly, the syllogism is of a form "All A is C (major premise), B is A (minor premise), so B is C (conclusion)." Consider the argument, for example, that all Greeks are philosophers, Socrates is Greek, ergo Socrates is a philosopher. The argument is valid, although we know the major premise is not true.

All categorical syllogisms consist of three statements (propositions): the major premise, the minor premise, and the conclusion, formally in that order but appearing in everyday language with variation. There are precisely three terms in the syllogism. The subject of the conclusion is the minor term, and the predicate of the conclusion is the major term. The middle term joins the two premises to make the argument. Above, Socrates is the minor term, philosophers the major term, and Greeks the middle term, which is pivotal in the argument but does not appear in the conclusion.

By convention, statements are typed A,E,I,O.[92] A statements are of the form "All S is P." E says "No S is P." I says "Some S is P." And O says "Some S is Not P." The form of argument is classified by the order of these statement types and the location of the middle term.[93] With four forms of major premise, multiplied by four forms of minor premise, by four forms of conclusion, and by four positions of the middle term, a product of 256 classes of syllogistic argument are created, some valid, some invalid. For example,

All birds are feathered;

(all) Robins are birds;

(all) Robins are feathered.

The middle term, birds, is in first position and the AAA1 argument is valid. But,

Some boxes are wood;

Some barrels are wood;

Some barrels are boxes.

The middle term, wood, is in second position and the III-2 argument is invalid. These forms, AAA-1 and III-2, are valid and invalid respectively, regardless of the content. It is the formalization, generality, and orderliness of syllogistic reasoning that fortified logic's creation. Its rules are an aid to critical evaluation of arguments, and a guide for decomposing elaborate, complex, and confused discourse.[94] These rules can be exposed in a variety of ways, such as the graphic displays of Venn diagrams.[95]

Syllogisms are arguments whose statements (propositions) are so constructed that, when correctly composed and arranged, conclusions are <u>necessarily</u> valid. Categorical statements consist of terms that are binary—that is, either yes or no, either included in a class or not.[96] For example, all dogs have paws, so there are no dogs without paws. Some dogs have fleas, so there must be some dogs with no (zero) fleas. No dogs have horns, so there are no dogs with horns.

In yet another form, the syllogism is employed to deal with conditional, or hypothetical, if-then statements. Such statements assert that a condition will exist only if certain pre-conditions exist and that there is non-ambiguous link. If all A are B, and if all B is C, then A is C. The hypothetical is stated or implied in much of scientific inquiry, as well as in ordinary life pursuits.

From Aristotelian times, indeed well before, the rules of reason were tested, criticized, corrected, and developed as a specialized branch of philosophy and a tool for virtually all of mankind. From early times, for example, the Stoics offered criticism of the Aristotelian system of reason, and an alternative that was, in later times, incorporated into a broader understanding of logic (Kneale and Kneale 1986, pp. 113-176). In recent times, general semantics challenged the binary quality of Aristotelian terms, as did "fuzzy logic," an alternative to classifying the world in terms of black/ white, yes/no, on/off, A and not-A.

## Fallacies

The abbreviated mention of the categorical syllogism above serves to illustrate human introspection about the thought process under the heading, logic. The syllogism provides the roots of a subdiscipline of philosophy with its own language (symbolic logic), support for its sibling (mathematics), and footing for its offspring such as science and law. While scholarly studies refine and extend the formal constructs of logic, the rules of argument applied to everyday life help identify errors, suggest corrections, and enlarge human knowledge. Some of these errors are lumped together and typed as "fallacies."

Formally, fallacy is simply invalidity posing as validity. A more casual way of putting it might be mistake, error, or untruth. Mistakes can be made in a variety of ways such as having one or more untrue premises. But an argument can be invalid even when premises are true, as when there is a logical or reasoning failure. Consider, for example, the argument guilty of circular reasoning. Here, one of the argument's premises is repeated as its conclusion, often disguised in ambiguous rhetoric. For example, (1) trust in a bank is essential for its economic success, (2) the unbridled confidence of the people is exhibited in their financial transactions every day, (3) economic success is the product of faith in the bank from its customers. Both premises and the conclusion could be true, but the conclusion is a rewording of the first premise and the argument is invalid.

Fallacies are generated in other ways, such as "false causes" where an event or condition is inferred from another event or condition simply because the first sequentially precedes the second. In scientific endeavor, correlation may be confused with cause/effect when variables are in a consistent sequential pattern. Logicians' texts classify and describe fallacies in a variety of ways. Copi, for example, references 112 fallacies, and describes 18 in detail, some earning fallacy status because of the irrelevance of premise to conclusion, some earning it by ambiguity where terms shift in meaning or contain more than one meaning (Copi, 1986, pp. 91-122).

Fallacies may be unintentional, due to inadequate attention to the structure of the argument, or intentional, a deliberate attempt to mislead. But no discussion of fallacy should fail to mention another source of untruth, indifference. If a statement, or set of statements, is presented solely to evoke some impression without concern for its truth, tests of logic do not apply. Orators and ad-writers have been known to stir emotions without any concern for the truth of statements or arguments using "humbug," "bunkum," or, in Professor Frankfurt's carefully defined terminology, "bullshit" (Frankfurt, 2005).

## Ideas of Mathematics

"The science of pure mathematics, in its modern developments, may claim to be the most original creation of the human spirit....The originality of mathematics consists ...[of]...connections between things...exhibited which, apart from the agency of human reason, are extremely unobvious." (Whitehead, 1956, p. 402)

The mathematics of which Whitehead wrote is easily conceived as an aspect or extension of logic. Or perhaps it is the other way around. Clearly, the deductive strategies employed in problem solution are similar, if not exactly the same. The notion of classes and categories is inherent in logical structures and mathematical equations. The language of inference is shared by logic and mathematics. They are sibling pursuits of mind.

It is not surprising that the historical development of thought in mathematics overlapped that of logic, and that both were related to the emergence of writing around 3000 BCE.[97] The Western development of mathematics over 4 millennia depended heavily on exchanges between and among the Hellenic, Arabic, and Indian cultures, and clearly improvements in writing materials and techniques aided in the exchanges.

The first step in the development of mathematics must have been numbering, or the conceptual leap from the ordinal smaller-bigger, shorter-longer, sooner-later type of relationships to discrete, cardinal numbers such as 1, 5, and 9.[98] This leap was made, most likely, well before the beginning of agriculture, but was refined and improved to meet the practical needs of trade, organization, and cultural growth. Numbering implies discrimination, classification, and grouping so, in a sense, it anticipates the qualities of a unit such as "A or Not-A," the basis of Aristotelian syllogisms asserted millennia later.

The second great step in mathematics was the development of a system of notation—the naming of numbers and arranging them in agreeable form for recording, communicating, and, critically, manipulating by arithmetic, geometry, and, eventually, modern mathematics. The efficiency of notation—e.g., the name "5" instead of "$1+1+1+1+1$"—was necessary for all but the simplest tasks of counting. While most mathematical expressions probably could be written in words, as are some sentences in logic, the shear volume and complexity of word numbers would disable all but the simplest arithmetic or algebra. The power—beauty, if you will—of mathematics is economy of expression. In that sense, mathematics is to logic what poetry is to prose.

Further developments in devising a numbering system included positioning, decimals, and zero. Sumerians had a fully developed numbering system, employing cuneiform figures, early in the second millennium BC. Its only deficiency was a lack of zero, which was brought to the region late in the first millennium.

From the earliest forms of quantification grew the applications and principles of arithmetic, geometry, algebra, and calculus.

Perhaps the longest mathematical stride was what we today take for granted—simple arithmetic.[99] Sums, differences, divisions, and multiples are powerful tools for commerce, production, and daily living, and little more need be said about these tools. Before leaving arithmetic, however, mention should be made of the concept that captures the moneylender's soul—compound interest. Compound interest is interest on interest over time. Very briefly: value at some time in the future depends on the rate of interest, periodicity of compounding, and length of time. In its most elemental form: $FV = PV (1 + i)^n$ where $n$ is the number of times interest is taken. This simple concept is a powerful tool to explain the amassing of wealth and can be generalized to other growth processes,[100] say, for population, food supply, energy, or money.

Compound interest is a special case of exponential functions widely used to define measure or display growth or decline. Exponentials capture the idea of accelerating growth or decline, as with bacteria, weeds, or rabbits. A common use of the exponential is tracing and projecting change in human population over time. The earth's human population[101] took more than 150,000 years to grow to 1 million at the beginning of civilization (agriculture, about 10,000 years ago). By the year 1800, there were 1 billion people on earth, by 1900 there were more than 1.6 billion, and by 2010 the population had grown to 7 billion.[102] These numbers illustrate the power of the exponential, stated in its most elemental form as $g(x) = b^x$ where b, the base, is fixed and x is a variable. This means that, however small x is to begin with, its accumulative power drives values such as the population numbers to very high figures.

As in other acts of human creation, mathematics has evolved over long periods of time, absorbing the thoughts and experiments of many people in widely distant places. Geometry, for example, evolved from the rudiments and rules of thumb that guided Egyptian essays[103] in practical geometry around 3000 BCE to the Pythagorean principles of 6th century BCE.[104] Pythagoras (584-495 BCE) was a renowned Grecian scholar whose works might be considered the Rosetta Stone for the abstractions of modern mathematics. His pupils formed a mystical Order of Pythagoreans involved in many areas of inquiry, notably medicine.[105] Today, Pythagoras is perhaps most widely known for his theorem that the area of a square of the hypotenuse equals the sum of squares of the legs of a right triangle.

Euclid (c. 325-265 BCE) set forth a body of principles that guided geometry for the following 2,000 years. His most noted achievement was *Elements*, a 13-volume work that amassed knowledge of geometry and its proofs to that point in history. Euclidean geometry[106] is a vision of space with proofs and methods of space measurement. Those methods of measurement, and their refinements, continue to underlie the inventions and constructs of modern life, be they contact lenses, skyscrapers, or space stations. The geometry used to re-measure and mark the boundaries of cultivators' plots erased by the flooding Nile in ancient times now helps to project the land surface likely to be submerged by waters rising from global warming.

Algebra extends the categorical relationships of logic to quantification, but without particular numbers. The equations of algebra state formulas of equalities that show how the size of one variable depends on the size of another. In the realm of thinking about thinking, therefore, algebra enables a test of reality (a numerical answer) that aids in criticism and correction. While algebraic formulations are found in Euclid's *Elements*, c. 300 BCE, and expanded extensively in Omar Khayyam's treatise on algebra, c.1100 CE, many puzzles and problems remained until a mathematical renaissance in the 17th and 18th centuries, led by Descartes, Leibniz, Newton, and Gauss.

Arithmetic, algebra, and geometry defined and quantified perceptions of form and structure. Numbers added precision to comparisons. Geometry explained space. Algebra expressed relationships between/among variables. Then Leibniz and Newton, in the late 17th and early 18th centuries, developed the calculus to specify and measure rates and amounts of change, such as the distance a falling object will travel in a specified interval of time.

Differential calculus addresses changes on the functional relations between independent variables. Its metric is derived from infinitesimal differences on the slopes of those functions. The calculation yields a derivative with respect to the variable under study and describes shapes of curves, velocities, trends, maxima, and minima in processes such as production, population, or erosion. In a simple, generalized form for the derivative (tiny change) in the functional relation of $y$ to $x$, that is, $y = f(x)$, the derivative (the tangent) at a point $x$ is $dy(x)/dx$. It is calculated for any $n$ as $d/dx\,(x^n)$ = $nx^{n-1}$. (If the relation $y = f(x)$ is constant, the derivative value is 0.) Integral calculus, somewhat the inverse of differential, is a summation of the minute changes under the slope of a curve describing the relation of $y$ (say, weight, jobs, or value) to $x$ (say, year, distance, or investment). Calculus underlies the development of modern technology, underpins the engineering design of the infrastructure, and models the organization of the economy and society. John von Neumann extols the eminence of the calculus in modern mathematics:

> "The calculus was the first achievement of modern mathematics, and it is difficult to overestimate its importance. I think it defines more unequivocally than anything else the inception of modern mathematics, and the system of mathematical analysis which is its logical development, still continues the greatest technical advance in exact thinking." (Neumann *in* Newman, 1956, pp. 2055-6)

Because of its significance to empirical research, another branch of mathematics—probability—deserves mention. Notions and even mathematical theories about probability underpin modern statistics and anticipate the methods of science.

One view of probability rests on an assumption of a deterministic universe, requiring of mathematical inquiry only a correct formulation of all objects and activity. The inability to make flawless prediction is only a knowledge deficit problem according to Laplace (1749-1827), one of the early students of probability (Hawking, 2005, pp. 386-7). Another view is that some randomness is inherent in the nature of the universe and, despite the appearance of some regularities, unexpected things happen. Ignoring the deeper philosophic aspects of probability, one might define it simply as the ratio of favorable (expected or observed) to possible in a specified set such as a statistical sample. Addressing practicalities, Nagel, in his "Meaning of Probability", writes that "...no theory can be established beyond every possibility of doubt by any finite number of observations" (Nagel, in Newman, 1956, p. 1401).

## Gnosis

Mathematics is, or can be, more than a mere tool in other intellectual pursuits such as astronomy, physics, or economics. Mathematics, in its frugality of expression, rigor, and council of relations, is a source of creativity in its own right. As Leslie White wrote in the *Locus of Mathematical Reality*:

"The locus of mathematical reality is cultural tradition i.e., the continuum of symbolic behavior...Ideas interact with each other in the nervous systems of men and thus form new syntheses. If the owners of these nervous systems are aware of what has taken place they call it invention as Hadamard does, or "creation," to use Poincare's term." (White, 1956, pp. 2363-4)

Imagine all knowledge collected as a sphere, stretchable like a balloon. An invention or creation inside the sphere ferments and knowledge grows. Old puzzles are solved, new relations are realized, discoveries are exposed, and the knowledge sphere grows. And as the volume of the knowledge sphere expands, so does its surface. At that surface, knowledge confronts the great void of knowledge, or ignorance. The more we know, the more we become aware of what is not known. And the calculus offers a neat way of defining it, namely, that the surface area of a sphere is the derivative of its volume. Of course, without some metric for measuring collected knowledge, the sphere and its volume/surface relationship is mere analogy—but perhaps an interesting way of using mathematics to express an epistemological thought or construct.

Knowledge may be just another way of defining "thinking about thinking." Even as he was composing his treatise on medicine, or honing his syllogisms, Aristotle was concerned about the way mankind acquires, extends, and alters knowledge. In *Posterior Analytics* he says: "The things we seek are equal in number to those we understand. We seek four things: the fact, the reason why, if it is, what it is" (Aristotle, in Ackrill, 1987, p. 50). From Aristotle another 1,000 years of knowledge accumulated to become the foundation of modern scientific thinking.

## Science

Thinking about thinking approached a pinnacle with the rise of science in the 17th and 18th centuries. But, as in other human creations, developments in the philosophy of science were buttressed by the works of earlier times, in particular, the enlightenment of 15th and 16th centuries. Emergence of science as a way of thinking was reflected in advances in understanding regarding the universe.[107] Curiosity and a critical mind brought forth Copernicus' challenge to the Ptolemaic concept of an earth-centered universe. In 1543, the year of his death, Nicholas Copernicus published the results of his study of planets,[108] stating that the earth and other planets rotated around the sun rather than the sun and planets rotating about the earth, a counterintuitive notion. Others before him concluded likewise,[109] but they were a scholarly minority—and a minority with an idea not well received by prevailing church authority at the time. Copernicus carefully worded his heliocentric explanation as "only a theory" and dedicated his book to the Pope in order to avoid a charge of heresy and its fiery consequences. Although his circular orbits and calculations were wrong, his insights and reasoning were an important link to advances in astronomy via Brahe, Kepler, Galileo, and Newton.

From Ptolemy's 1st century description of the universe until Copernicus, the geocentric approach was generally unchallenged either in terms of a deductively conceived model or carefully designed reality test, the two basic elements of science. The official Christian Church was satisfied with an earth-centered model for its creation story. Meanwhile, Islamic scholars, integrating and improving on Greek thinking, helped prepare the groundwork for the Copernican revolution. Tyco Brahe,[110] a generation after Copernicus, improved the Copernican model, but perpetuated some Ptolemaic shortcomings. Tyco mentored Johannes Kepler and corresponded with Galileo Galilei, who resisted Tyco's efforts to convince him of some old geocentric assumptions.

Kepler, in 1609, described the elliptical motions of the planets, including distances and speeds, thus providing much of the foundation of modern astronomy. Kepler suggested, but did not explain, the nature of forces holding the universe together, leaving that task to Isaac Newton in his theory of universal gravitation published in *Principia* in 1687.[111]

Galileo, a contemporary of Kepler, is renowned for publishing his heliocentric explanation of celestial position and motion, based on observations from a telescope of his design, and for contributions to the law of acceleration of falling bodies and the mathematical properties of matter. Bertrand Russell called Galileo the greatest of the founders of modern science, with the possible exception of Newton, noting his birth on the day of Michelangelo's death, and death on the day of Newton's birth (Russell, 1945, p. 531). However, from the standpoint of thinking about thinking, Galileo is best known for his role in the clash between religion and science. Following his trial by the Inquisition, many of Galileo's writings were suppressed or destroyed, and he died in 1642 still under house arrest.

Galileo (1564-1642) lived in a turbulent era, and not only in scholarship. He was born just 47 years after Martin Luther sparked a Christian Reformation with his famous 95 theses, and died shortly before the end of the Thirty Years War. During his lifetime,

Harvey lectured and published on blood circulation. The King James Bible was published in 1611, in the midst of Shakespeare's dramatic achievements. North America was being explored, settled, and fought over.

Francis Bacon, born just 3 years before Galileo, brought to the scientific revolution an emphasis on induction, or reasoning from fact to explanation. His method contrasted with deduction, or reasoning from premises to conclusion. Bacon's scientific method was directed against the dominance of thinking in Aristotelian, syllogistic terms. Bacon's *Novum Organum* shifted the balance from syllogistic reasoning to insights drawn from observation—another step in science where logical construct dances with empirical test. Each partner in that dance both challenges and supports the other's expression and strengths.

From the enormous expansion of scientific knowledge in the 17th and 18th centuries grew the 19th century technological transformations in industry, exploration, transportation, communication, and organization. Perhaps in response to a world driven to doing, growing, making, and accumulating, philosophers recharged their interest in thinking about thinking. Early in the 20th century, for example, logical positivism became a notable feature in the philosophy of science.[112] The logical positivists emphasized verifying the truth of propositions by sense experience, and rejecting anything considered as having value content. Their notion of verifiability contributed substantially to the clarity of science.

However, in response to the rigidity and extremes of the logical positivist community, Karl Popper (1902-1994), a distinguished philosopher of science, turned verifiability toward a more modest test of falsifiability which requires that a hypothesis be so stated that it *can* fail a test. A "successful" hypothesis, then, is one that is not proven wrong, while recognizing that no hypothesis can be ever proven right.[113] The falsifiability criterion provides a built-in humility to scientific achievement.

The human condition is beset with change. When paced incrementally (slowly), it is called evolution. When sudden or drastic, it can be called revolution. So it has been attended by historians of the many professions. For example, Joseph Schumpeter (1883-1950), wrote about change in capitalism:

"Capitalism, then, is by nature a form or method of economic change and not only never is but never can be stationary...the capitalist engine in motion comes from the new consumers' goods, the new methods of production or transportation, the new markets, the new form of industrial organization that capitalist enterprise creates." (Schumpeter, 1976, pp. 82-83)

Schumpeter lumped such changes in the economy under the term "creative destruction." Similar changes in the intellectual world of science were called "paradigm shifts" by Thomas Kuhn in his widely cited *The Structure of Scientific Revolutions* (Kuhn, 1996).[114] Paradigm shifts are a form of scientific revolution that is contrasted with the slower, sustained, step-by-step concept of evolution.[115] Kuhn writes: "...scientific revolutions are here taken to be those non-cumulative developmental episodes in which an older paradigm is replaced in whole or in part by an incompatible new one." (Kuhn, 1996, p. 92)

As he nears the climax of his argument, Kuhn turns to the Darwinian perspective on the origin of species. The paradigm shift was not the long evolutionary process of the life process itself—it had been described for decades. It was the way Darwin perceived it, that is, not some goal directed plan (with mankind the center of it), but an adaptive process of competition, natural selection, and survival. The attention, turmoil, and concern with Darwin's paradigm were not the subject matter of the science but the implications of his methodology. In the Darwin story, as elsewhere, Kuhn's insistence on a revolutionary tone adds drama to the story of scientific discovery. It also allows the personification of additions to human knowledge, even though all but the least modest discoverer attributes success to those who have gone before.

Nonetheless, the fruits of technology—based on science, mathematics and statistics—have had an enormous influence on the well-being and survival of humans. Clearly, among the earth's living things, brainpower has been humans' competitive edge, enabling their growth to 7 billion. The downside has been an increasing dependence on science to replace the slower, but perhaps more durable, management by nature, that is, the replacement of self-correcting little screw-ups with planetary disaster. Turning back is not an option. Hopefully logic will self-correct.

# Writing

"...by far the most important step in the passage to civilization was writing." (Durant)[116]

Writing is commonly credited for advancing human organization by bridging people's communications in time and space. As such, writing reduces uncertainty. A contract or agreement symbolized with mutually understood marks on/in some permanent medium becomes a vital instrument of commerce. If that medium is easily portable, transactions can take place between distant parties. Beyond commerce, writing enables a sharing of reasoning, reflections, and sentiments at distances and over time. Writing provides a degree of permanence to an idea or expression, an aid to memory. The extension of human knowledge would be extremely limited without the means of recording the ideas and experiences of others—and retaining one's own thoughts and intuitions.

In the advance of civilization, a vital, indeed defining, quality of writing is its ability to clarify ideas and statements. Writing enables error detection for reflection and correction.

## Origins

As in other human creations, the origins of writing cannot be assigned a solitary, unambiguous time, place, or person. In part, this is a problem of definition. Did early scratches on a stick or bone, presumably for counting, constitute writing? Or Paleolithic cave paintings? Earliest writing could be more properly credited to pottery markings and mercantile symbols well after the beginnings of agriculture. Commerce encouraged the keeping of records, hence writing. Antecedents of present-day writing are probably no older than 3500 BCE. Writing and history are mutually defined in the sense that history relies largely on written records, using archeological information only to support written evidence. "Pre-history" means pre-writing.

Writing first appeared in Mesopotamia and surrounding areas at a time of rapidly developing settlement and commerce. One of the earliest forms of writing was the Bronze Age cuneiform, wedge-shaped markings pressed into clay. The oldest of these relics appear to have been for counting, suggesting writing's emergence as a supplement to commercial activity and belying the notion that creations are born of mere tinkering and not necessity.

Dating and placing the origins of writing is subject to much scholarly debate, partly due to classification of forms and criteria for inclusion. For example, cave carvings in China have been dated 7 to 8 millennia ago, yet by most generally accepted criteria, Chinese writing appeared about 3500 years ago. Pictographic systems such as the Egyptian hieroglyphics existed in the pre-history era, that is, before the late 4th millennium BCE. Writing as we know it began in Sumer around 3100 BCE. Cuneiform markings were at first symbols of things and ideas, and later developed into alphabetic respresentations of spoken language. Sumerian cuneiform was adapted to the spoken language writing system by Akkadians, Assyrians, and Babylonians during the 3rd millennium BCE. However, not until

1400 BCE, in Mycenae, Greece, was a script designed solely on the sound structure of language.[117]

As point of reference, writing came into being long after the beginning of agriculture. Without writing, the advances in industry, commerce, medicine, and logic would have been impossible. Writing enabled survival of the species, and writing also enabled literature and its offspring arts without which survival would have been meaningless.

## Forms

In simplest terms, writing is a visual communication system in two general forms: direct, as a symbol for an object, action, or idea; and indirect, as a symbol for the sound of a verbal expression of the object, action, or idea. Examples of the first are ancient cave paintings or Chinese logographics. Examples of the second are Hindi and English. To offset visual impairment, symbols may be tooled, as in Braille, for sense of touch. The two basic forms are further classified into groups by linguistic and stylistic refinements. For example, some writing systems such as Arabic or Hebrew use symbols only for consonants, while others such as Cyrillic and English use symbols for both consonants and vowels. Further variations arise with symbols for combinations of syllables, inflections, sounds, and tones. Some writing such as Hebrew and Greek has been developing over long periods of time, while others such as Cherokee and Thai have developed only recently.

The forms and methods of writing are determined by available technology and materials. The pictographs on cave walls were made possible by charcoal easily obtained from the fires that illuminated the walls. The walls, in turn, protected the pictographs from erasure by the elements. Colors could be added from earth minerals like iron oxide and ochre, and from vegetable dyes. Also, representations in relief could be achieved by chiseling or plastering. Pictographs have been dated thousands of years before the modern (agricultural) era, much preceding the age of symbols for sound/spoken language.

Egyptian hieroglyphs of common objects such as an arm, bird, or reed represent either a concept or a sound, and symbolize the evolution from pure pictographs toward phonemes and alphabet. Mostly, these hieroglyphs were carved in stone for permanence, not portability. Around 3100 BCE, the Egyptians soaked, pounded, and dried specially arranged papyrus reed strips into a paperlike writing material well suited for documentation and portability. The process was so highly valued that it was kept secret for centuries. Papyrus greatly enhanced the scope and content of communications among Egyptians and their correspondents.

Cuneiform and clay have a natural affinity. Clay is abundant and easily formed into tablets for inscription with a simple writing tool. The cuneiform inscriptions consist of collections of wedge-shaped marks in various positions and combinations. By 2500 BCE, the cuneiform had evolved in Mesopotamia to a refined system and it continued to develop through 500 BCE and the great Persian Empire.[118] The Code of Hammurabi for governing the people of Babylonia, written about 1790 BCE, was one of the first legal documents in writing.

Paper developed in China. About 105 BCE, T'sai Lun in the court of Emperor Ho Tsi invented the process of papermaking. He made a slurry of crushed plant fibers that, when laid out in a thin film and dried, became a light, durable, flexible sheet of paper. Papermaking migrated to several Asian countries, then to the West in the 8th century CE. Paper as a material had a thousand uses, most significantly as a medium for writing with the arrival of the Gutenberg press in 1440 CE and the democratization of literacy. Even at the height of the Renaissance, however, books were rare. The University of Cambridge in 1473 had about 330 volumes (Oates, 1975). Individual holdings were small, and affordable by only a few.

Paper at first was a milestone in saving space and easing access to ideas, but in time it also became burdensome and susceptible to damage. The Library of Congress collection was only 3,000 books, for example, when it was burned by the British in the War of 1812.[119] The current LOC collection contains 32 million catalogued books and 62 million manuscripts. The sheer bulk of books and other printed materials is being condensed by new storage and transmission technology.

Electronics are the latest evolutionary step in communication. Early in the 19th century, Samuel Morse, building on experiments of others, invented the first telegraph capable of transmitting dot-dash signals over wire. By the mid- 19th century, Elisha Gray and Alexander Bell were competing to patent sound devices—telephones—to transmit speech over wire. These inventions began an evolution toward media capable of transmitting visual and audible signals around and off the planet, instantly, and storing messages in very small spaces, to be recovered easily and quickly. That evolution is still underway, with consequences for human organization yet unknown. Writing remains an important feature of human evolution and, while competing for human attention with other forms of sound and sight signals, probably will remain the basic tool for expressing and developing the ideas needed for civilization.

## Language

"Language is a completely arbitrary symbol of thought. Writing is a symbol of the spoken language, less arbitrary than the language itself, since in most systems of writing there is an attempt to make characters correspond to sounds. A system of writing is a symbol of a symbol, just as a check is symbolical of paper money, which is in turn symbolical of gold." (Pei, 1965, p. 90)

Underlying writing is language, broadly defined as the mechanism of communicating. Writing includes only a portion of the language mechanism. A language in use includes gestures, facial expressions, motions, and poses. In other words, much depends upon what is regarded as language, as evidenced by the communication modes among other species.[120] Human language incorporates a large body of conventions, traditions, and understandings not always visible in written signs and symbols. Writing to members outside a cult or to translation can differ radically from writing to insiders, and in the long run will spur adaptations.

When people are widely separated and formed in insular clans, languages will be many and distinct. As contacts increase and communities enlarge, languages will merge and some will change or disappear. Writing is complicated by the large number of languages, many rapidly becoming extinct. Half of the current 6,000 languages will be gone by the end of the century.[121] Most on the planet will communicate in a half dozen or so of the major languages such as Mandarin, English, or Arabic. Storage and translation of the historically significant content of dead and receding languages is a major challenge.

Clearly, there is a tradeoff between preservation of separate languages and the universal use of a single language. The immediate, direct advantages of a universal language are obvious for social, economic, religious, and political intercourse. The creation and promotion of the ethnically neutral Esperanto language, for example, was intended to reduce the barriers to communication across national, ethnic borders. Its failure was due, in part at least, to its objective of ethnic neutrality, leapfrogging the cultural heritage of a separate language. The universal adoption of English has some of the same drawbacks as Esperanto, but otherwise comes closest to a universal language with some good reasons.[122] Failing some formal international policy, current trends point to the extinction of many languages and adoption of a few, or one, international language. However, writing, supported by translation, will help preserve the heritage of disappearing languages.

## Literacy

Writing, of course, implies reading. The critical feature of writing is an agreement of communicators about the meaning of signs and symbols. And the effectiveness of a writer's message will be a function of the number or portion of intended readers that will correctly grasp the message. That means literacy.

The ability to read a newspaper is but one definition of literacy, albeit a practical and accommodating one. However, it does not measure levels of comprehension or speed of absorption, nor does it take into account the breadth of material available for reading. As recently as the 15$^{th}$ century, despite the technical advancements in printing, only a small portion of the population could afford the luxury of a book. Where available at all, the Bible was basic reading material. A "renaissance person" of the 17$^{th}$ century would have read a dozen classics, a newspaper, and a few broadsides, while his modern counterpart will have digested hundreds of classics, the contents of professional journals, blogs, periodicals, and countless other publications. Worldwide, illiteracy appears to be declining, but this decline may be due in part to a standard not revised to reflect the volume and immediacy of present-day writing.

In less developed countries, many people are unschooled, and deprived of reading materials. In developed countries, alliteracy, or choosing not to read, is common enough to be a source of social, economic, and democratic dysfunction. Economic deprivation may account for some of the alliteracy in developed countries, but given the massive opportunities for free access to all forms of print, much of it can be attributed to electronic substitutes. Television, barely a half century old, is the modern-day equivalent to cave pictures. Cell phones can now bypass transmission wires and do the work of cameras, geo-positioners, text messagers, calculators, calendars, and even translators. Miniature storage devices hold enormous quantities of words and numbers. Small hand-held readers contain huge libraries. The rapidly evolving world of electronic devices provides dizzying opportunities for either enhancing or replacing writing. What will it be? [123]

At present, there is neither a truly universal language nor script. Nearest approximations would be the language of mathematics and binary code, or perhaps music and musical notation. Mathematical symbols may represent a "natural" language of conditions, patterns, and operations that are universal. The numbers and signs might appear in different script, but concepts are universal. The binary code is universal to modern electronic operations. The now common musical notation shows pitch as oval symbols of notes placed on or between five horizontal lines of a staff. Tempo is guided by measures marking off the staff with vertical bars. This form was established in the late 16th-early 17th century and is now virtually universal.

## For Composition

Writing is a remarkable achievement...but what's it for?

The mechanics of writing has been emphasized thus far, so a note on the content of writing is in order. A literate society demands more than the mere elements of language formation such as alphabet, medium,[124] means of storage, and punctuation. The driving force of language and writing is composition, the transformation of ideas into visible or tactile records to inform, entertain, imagine, and inspire. James Madison's Constitution, Shakespeare's *King Lear*, Homer's *Odyssey*, Adam Smith's *Wealth of Nations* and thousands of other exemplars of organization, morals, and sentiment are the stuff of writing. The stuff is what writing is for.

## Scripture

For a person unschooled in written communication, words rising from a page or tablet could easily seem divinely inspired, or divinely dictated. For many in the literate world, also, the written word carries spiritual authority. It is not surprising, then, that the great religions of the world are supported by, or based on, one or more written documents. The Abrahamic religions (Christianity, Judaism, Islam), representing over half of the world's population, base their faith directly on divine scripture. Indeed, Islam recognizes as authentic only scripture in its original language—that many of its adherents do not understand. Christians, too, worshiped divine words in Latin, requiring priestly intervention to translate and interpret, until the reform movement initiated translations into common languages.

In the Bible's story of the Exodus, for example, it is significant that Moses, after his 40 days on Mt. Sinai, emerged with the ten commandments written on stone tablets. The tablets were stone for permanence and durability, and *written* to enhance authority. Moses might have delivered God's message orally, but the story emphasized that the message was inscribed—on stone.

Scripture's authority confers power. Torah, Bible, Koran. Much of the power in that authority flows from moral persuasion to individuals directly "from the word." More often, the persuasiveness flows from interpretations produced by scholars, priests, authors, and promoters who, intimately or distantly, comprise the bureaucracy of religion.

But why would any divine authority elect to demand exclusive allegiance and issue moral imperatives in writing? Clearly, writing's superiority over speech in preservation and critical evaluation is helpful in worldly communication, but with complete and universal power over all, writing would seem unnecessary. Furthermore, most of the 200 millennia of human existence has been without divine instruction in writing. Why then would the Commandments be presented in writing to Judaism in 1400 BCE?[125] In the beginning was the word, but the need for it to appear in writing appears to be of very recent vintage.

Nevertheless, the written scripture appears to carry a great deal of weight among a very large number of people. Historically, holy books have occupied a prominent position in household libraries around the world.

But authoritative text is not limited to religious scripture. Codes, constitutions, contracts, and scholarly articles are non-religious works enhanced, or preserved, by writing. These documents too have their legal, economic, and literary bureaucracies, and their constituencies. All trade in authority. All acquire or grant power. All depend upon the organizing force of the written word.

## Writing and Knowledge

Detection, reflection, correction, however encrypted, are stages in the creation process. Writing has been critical in human exposure to information for detection. The technologies of encoding, transmission, and decoding have greatly hastened, enlarged, and cheapened access to information. In the lifetimes of even our youngest, we humans have witnessed the exponential growth in information floating around in a variety of forms.

The good news about writing is its growth in capacity to generate, exchange, and store information needed for an organized presence of 7 billion people on earth. The bad news is that the 7 billion have left much of that capacity unused or misused. Lessons relating to unchecked population growth, for example, are more accessible but no better heeded.

Technology has mightily expanded the exposure to data, facts, and experiences—the ingredients for detection. The challenge now is reflection. We face the problem not of data, but of coherence.

# God

"If God did not exist, it would be necessary to invent him."
Voltaire

"...we shall all, philosophers, scientists, and just ordinary
people, be able to take part in the discussion of the question
of why it is that we and the universe exist. If we find the answer
to that, it would be the ultimate triumph of human reason—for
then we would know the mind of God."
Stephen Hawking[126]

In the same way that nature abhors a vacuum, humans feel driven
to explain the unexplained, to solve mysteries and to untangle
befuddlements. Not surprisingly, then, we see a long history of
explanations as to why and how we humans came to exist, and why
and how the universe within which we came to exist came to exist.
If we are to describe human creations, it is reasonable to have an
explanation for how and why we human creators are created.

Religion generally, and God specifically, provides explanations
both metaphysical—for how we came to be—and moral, for how
we ought to be. An explanation of existence, or creation, can be the
source of great authority. That authority, in turn, may be the basis

for exercising control over behavior. While the usefulness of moral doctrines or ethical premises can be argued without resort to transcendent consequences administered by God, history has shown widespread search for, and acceptance of, a highest (even if invisible) authority. The search for and interpretation of that authority, as in other creative processes, became specialized as doctrine and codified as occupation.

## In the Beginning

Creation stories abound. They are an important feature of most if not all cultures, and their diversity usually can be associated with a habitat, occupation, unusual event, or experience of the early storytellers and their followers. Creation stories generally begin with a form of void, emptiness, chaos, or primordial soup.[127]

Norsemen, for example, trace their mythical beginnings to an enormous abyss from which beginnings emerge. The abyss notion could be an imaginary extension of rugged mountains plunging into the depths of northern fjords, crevasses in glaciers, or depths of icy northern seas. From the abyss, or *ginnungagap*, heat and cold intermingle to form frost, from which issues Ymir, the frost giant, who in turn forms male and female giants. Three of Ymir's descendants ultimately kill him, and from those remains spring earth, plants, and creatures. Asgard functions as a heaven-like place from which all the Norse gods observe their work of creating earth's features and creatures.

The Norse gods and goddesses[128], like Greek gods and goddesses, were specialists, each assigned a particular aspect of the believer's life and experience. Thor was the thunder god, Tyr the god of war, Freya the goddess of sex and fertility, Freyr the god of weather, and Loki the giant god of thieves.

Odin was head of the Aesir family of gods and goddesses. Odin and fellow gods, Hoenir and Lodur, created man from one tree and woman from another. To the ancient Norsemen, trees were an abundant, viable building material, so timber would seem a natural origin for humans—creativity begins with the stuff at hand. Creation, by way of woodworking, would seem a likely match for a people with wood skills and traditions.

An interesting aspect of the Norse myth of creation is that the great abyss at the center of the fiery, frigid universe gives rise to the gods, rather than the other way around. Thus, not all creation stories begin with God as initiator.

As the ancient (pagan) Norsemen entered the Viking Age (roughly 1200 to 700 BCE), they encountered other cultures... and other creation stories. Some of these cultures practiced Christianity, with its version(s) of the creation story. One early encounter Viking with Christianity was the sacking of Lindisfarne in Scotland. Nevertheless, the Vikings trended toward Christianity so that by the $2^{nd}$ millennium CE, Christianity had become the national religion of Sweden.[129]

Two dozen and one creation stories have been collected and told by Virginia Hamilton in her *In the Beginning*.[130] In a cosmic egg-type story, for example, Phan Ku the Creator bursts from a universe shaped like a hen's egg to become the first being. He immediately grows to giant proportions and lives thousands of years in shaping the heavens and earth. Phan Ku self-destructs, and his remains form Earth. From his fleas, humans emerge. In another cosmic egg story, the Tahitian creator, Ta-aroa, bursts from his egg cosmos and immediately creates a companion god, Ti-I, with whom he creates the universe, man, and woman.

The Blackfoot American Indians saw the creator as an old man traveler constantly fashioning things such as prairies, rivers, birds, and animals. He makes a mother and child from clay, leaves them, and returns to find them. Each day they change until eventually they become as humans are now. The woman asks the old traveler whether humankind will be immortal. The answer: if a stone floats. As instructed, she throws a stone into the river and, upon its sinking, has her answer.

In Greek mythology, Prometheus' theft of fire from Zeus bestows on man great power to offset the superior physicality of the animals that Prometheus and his brother Epimetheus had created. With fire, man could make weapons, tools, and money, as well as warm his home. Prometheus felt rather clever, but Zeus was irritated and decided to best Prometheus. Zeus, with the aid of Venus, Mercury, and Apollo, assembled the new creation, wrapped it in innocence, and sent it the brothers Prometheus and Epimetheus whose creation, man, was completely upstaged and overpowered by... woman.

The last of creation myths in Hamilton's book is the story familiar to Judaism, Christianity, and Islam. The biblical account of creation is intended less as an explanation of creation or existence and more as a proclamation of God's glory and power. Hence, God appears as the cause of creation. Genesis does not explain how God came into being. "In the beginning God created the heavens and earth..."(Gen 1.l), and immediately the six-day creation project is underway.[131] In the biblical account, anthropocentrism reigns. Humankind is created "in our image."[132] Humankind is instructed to be fruitful and multiply, and to have dominion over everything that moves on earth.

In the beginning was the Word (John 1:1), but then there was the eraser. The Genesis story implies that creators sometimes make mistakes (Gen 6:5), re-evaluate (Gen 6:7), and self-correct (Gen 7: 11-16). That mirrors the human model of detection, reflection, and correction. Perhaps the biblical flood is the original account of a Schumpeterian "creative destruction."

Creation stories, and the beliefs associated with them, reduce uncertainty in believers by explaining existence and its many qualities. As such, the creation stories satisfy curiosity and ease anxieties about the unknown. But the creation stories also establish a source of power and authority in one of the many forms of God. Whether the product or agent of a great force as in the abyss, or originating source as in Genesis, God or gods and goddesses are vested with authority and are part of the legitimacy features of belief systems.

In the presence of the unknown, God is called upon to describe what is and prescribe what ought to be.

## After Creation, What?

Existence extends beyond arrival. That extension, for humans and their earthly companions, is labeled life. Midas Dekkers opens his provocative *The Way of All Flesh* (1997) by describing the life process as a stairway, but a stairway ascending to a high point and then descending to death.[133] For Dekkers, the stairway metaphor illustrates life's roles and responses, and indicates the importance of decay and death in the continuity of a species or life form. It is thus related to the notion of circularity, as manifest in reincarnation concepts.

One of the more durable sources of mystery and concern is death, or more precisely what happens to a person after death beyond mortal decay. It is the subject of much speculation and declaration, but with little (some would say no) consensus or veri- fication. The consequences of death are highly uncertain, so it is contemplated with much fear and apprehension, all of which makes "afterlife" conjectures more profound and ponderous. An eternal afterlife in heaven or hell surely must exert a strong influence on lifetime choices and moral bearings.[134]

The afterlife may also depend upon one's perception of the func- tions of God and the individual's relation thereto. God may be per- ceived as lifelong observer and accountant, post-mortem judge, and the administrator of one's final destination. The Christian notion of grace—the divine equivalent to forgiveness— ameliorates a strict earthly adherence to rules.

In broadest terms, there are two general categories of afterlife: (1) the projection of soul (and perhaps corporeal body) into some perpetual state of *paradise or damnation*, as espoused by Christians and Muslims, in which God figures; and (2) a rotational state of *reincarnation*, as held by Buddhists and Hindus, in which successive forms of existence rely largely on the state of one's mind, with God absent in Buddhism and pluralistic in Hinduism.

## Good and Evil, Ethics, Rules

The idea of creation implies a bringing of order out of disorder or chaos. That order further implies continuity, a regularity or predictability whether in nature—as in the seasons, animal growth, and gravity—or in human organization, as in governance, production, and religion. Nature and humanity have their laws that can be ignored at the risk of discomfort or peril. Jumping from a high bridge or driving through a red light can result in unpleasant consequences for the doer and possibly others. Hence, knowing laws and modifying behavior accordingly are essential. As human numbers increased, and intercourse became more complex, whole departments of rules with mechanics of implementation and enforcement became necessary not only to prevent anarchy and chaos but also to promote the ease and comfort of order. The religion department is about particular rules, their understanding, acceptance and enforcement. Some of those rules pertain to human conduct; other rules pertain to allegiance and obeisance to keepers and enforcers of the rules.

Rules are generally set in a framework of right and wrong, good and evil. Origins of evil are sometimes part of the creation story, like the fruit-eating story of disobedience in Genesis 3. Satan, in the form of a serpent, proffered fruit from the tree of knowledge to human #2, Eve.[135] She ate, Adam ate, God found out and worried they were on the slippery slope to becoming godlike and, heaven forbid, immortal. One can only imagine the mess created by humans being "fruitful and multiplying" as well as immortal. So God cast them out from what would have been for them, paradise. The fall of Adam and Eve through knowledge of good and evil clearly implies the primal role of rule setting in religion.

In the very broadest terms, the institution of religion consists of two complementary elements: a body of behavioral rules supported by a moral creed, and a moral authority to which members give reverence and power. The Ten Commandments encompass the two elements in a variety of forms and translations, but each appears to have about the same weight. First in order, God is quoted as claiming authority and requiring a number of rituals by worshipers to demonstrate their fealty to God and rejection of other gods. The second set[136] of elements is rules of behavior summed as a moral code. That moral code prescribes a social order and environment helpful to institutional continuity and, at a more basic level, human survival and well-being.

Uncertainty and unknowns are always present in everyday living, so means of coping are sought. For some, God fills that need. But what (who) is God?

Imago Dei. It is not surprising that some architect(s) of God would choose as a model for creation the most exalted of all creatures—*me* (us). Of course, humility would require the creation to be reversed, i.e., God created wonderful *me* (us) in his image (Gen. 1:26).[137] Then there is a difference between a personal God intimately tied to the behavior, even motivations, of each person and an impersonal God as sum of all the forces that impact on mankind and occur without concern for any particular individual. The personal image would seem to call for more direct relation, as in prayer and worship. The impersonal image might emphasize wonder and reflection, perhaps approaching the view of the humanist.

## The Interventions and God

*Agriculture*

"...agriculture and religion seem to have been intertwined since their respective invention." (Falvey, 2005, p. 12)

Adam, for his transgression, was expelled from the easy life of paradise and forever bound to toil as a farmer and suffer thorns and thistles to "eat the plants of the field." God said: "By the sweat of your face you shall eat bread until you return to the ground, for out of it you were taken." (Gen. 3:18-19) So the connection of God to agriculture was made early in the Judeo-Christian creation story. The closeness of agriculture to climatic, seasonal, weather, and pest conditions is a natural connection to powerful forces seemingly beyond the control of farmer or herdsman. However, having eaten of the tree of knowledge, humans devised clever interventions to enhance the desired, or deflect the unwanted, effects of nature. Selective breeding, cultivation, rotation, fertilization, irrigation, storage, and other agricultural techniques were employed; and over time were studied, critiqued, traded, and modified. Wisely, the agriculturists understood that not all hazards can be avoided or countered, so they undertook forms of insurance, such as saving for a rainy (or droughty) day, or sharing risks with an insurer. But despite all the growing, harvesting, saving, and insuring strategies, the forces of nature endure and surprise. All these forces may be included under God.

Other traditions honor the critical role of agriculture in human survival and, as such, the awe accorded the mysterious forces of nature. Demeter, goddess of grain and harvest, is prominent in the pantheon of Greek gods and goddesses. Seasonal festivals were celebrated in her honor. Before land was prepared for sowing, prayers were offered for a good harvest. Then Demeter Chloe was honored at a festival Chloia, at about the time that grain sprouts—perhaps a precursor to Lent. At harvest, the threshing floor celebration took place, followed later by a festival of thanksgiving. Notably, in pantheistic worship agriculture and earth—e.g., Gaia—were designated as female, perhaps to symbolize fertility and abundance.

Many ancient religions of the Amerindians were also polytheistic. And among the gods and goddesses were those with specific authority in agriculture. Mayan culture and religion, for example, was built around agriculture, notably corn, and overseen by Ah Mun, the god of corn. Similarly, the Aztec economy was organized around agriculture and corn, with central roles held by the god of corn, Centeotl, and his female counterpart, Chicomecoatl, the goddess of fertility. Hunter-gatherer nations and tribes tended to base their religions less on abstract gods and more on the daily world on which their survival depended. The Dakotas, for example, saw a spiritual dimension in their relationship to the buffalo. The Mandans, with a mixed agriculture and hunting culture, had rituals appropriate to planting and buffalo hunting. Commonly, the features of nature were assigned particular spiritual qualities.

Religions more closely associated with the spiritual qualities of directly sensed things such as the sun, serpent, wolf, or willow tree will be less oriented toward a supreme being. The human is more likely just another being in the plenary of beings. The afterlife is more likely associated with features of the here and now, and not a transcendence to some abstract heaven. In essence, death becomes an aspect of life and sustainability. It is this feature of sustainability[138] that is the principal theme of Lindsay Falvey's (2005) comparison of Christianity and Buddhism in agriculture and life processes generally. Buddhism does not entail a sovereign creator and ruler (God). Buddhism is a philosophy with rules aimed at personal enlightenment, and in that sense differs as a "religion" from Christianity and other Abrahamic faiths. Further, the scriptural instruction to Christians to dominate nature appears at variance to Buddhist instruction to understand and ally with natural forces. As a practical matter, either "stewardship" or a "oneness with nature" could lead to sustainable agricultural practices. Likewise, either a ruinous application of dominion or a lapse from one of the steps in the eightfold path could be a breach of sustainability. The form of religion may not result in different real world behavior—necessarily.

*Fire*

"Fire, which was crucial to civilized society, was also a god, and the Aryans called him *Agni*. Agni was not simply the divine patron of fire: he *was* the fire that burned in every single hearth." (Armstrong, 2006, p. 4)

Fire was a human tool long before humans lived in civilized (agricultural) society. Forms of reverence before the time of agriculture are still open to discovery and speculation, but if there were forces that were worshiped in pre-history times, surely fire would have been one of them. The great fireball, Ra, was believed by Egyptians to be creator and controller of the universe, for example. Fire and all its descendants of energy were instruments in human dominion of earth. Ritual incense, forge of the crusader's sword, funeral pyre—all are energized by fire. The many forms of fire virtually define the cultures of the world and their religious stories and rituals. Two examples— one ancient, one modern—show the span of faith and fire.

During the 2nd millennium BCE, the pastoral Aryans of the steppes north of the Caucuses learned to use fire to forge bronze tools and weapons. Fire already held an esteemed, even godly, position in their culture. Fire gave them new power. Horses were domesticated and added to the Aryans' mobility and power. The Aryans developed a capacity for plunder based on the mobility of the horse, not unlike the Vikings who used shipbuilding and sailing skills to raid and pillage. The Aryans were terrifying warriors who greatly expanded their territory of influence throughout the Middle East and India. Eventually, a portion of them sought a more peaceful and meaningful livelihood. They came under the influence of the Zarathustra[139] (c.1400-1200 BCE), a prophet teaching the supremacy of Ahura Mazda, god of worshipers in the Persian Empire from the 6th century BCE to the 7th century CE. The monotheistic Zarathustrianism had many elements absorbed later by Judaism, Christianity, and Islam.[140]

Contrasted with earlier Aryan/Iranian religions, Zarathustra emphatically asserted one god, Ahura Mazda (roughly translated as Lord Wise), creator and supreme being in a universe of two basic forces, Good (Spenista Mainyu) and Evil (Angra Mainyu). Ahura Mazda, under the name Ohrmazd, was equated with Good, in opposition to the dark Evil called Ahriman. The Good force is reflected in the overriding principle of the Zarathustrian religion: *Good Thoughts, Good Words, Good Deeds.* The Mazda "wise" implies far more than old-clever; it is closer to "enlightened," "brilliant," or "all-knowing"—perhaps as fire enlightens its surroundings.

The central icon of Zarathustrianism is fire.[141] This fire transcends not only the many meanings of warmth, but also illumination, energy, life force. As stated, fire was held in high esteem by ancestors of the Zarathustris, and that esteem was extended and formalized in their religion. Fire is, in the words of Roshan Rivetna, "a visible symbol of the divine, and of the inner light, the divine spark that burns within each individual. It is a physical representation of the illumined mind, enlightenment and truth—all concepts elevated to central importance by Zarathustra" (Rivetna, 2002, p. 37). Fire is incorporated in the religion's rituals, many conducted in the places of worship, the fire temples. The Zarathustrian community has shrunk from the dominant religion in the whole of the Persian empire to less than 280,000 today, primarily in Iran and India.

Quite another perspective on power, energy, and fire was drawn by Henry Adams in the "Dynamo and Virgin" chapter of his autobiographical *Education of Henry Adams*. From the dynamo exhibit in the 1900 Paris Exposition, historian Adams compares power from modern technology and from spiritual sources. Technology is expressed symbolically as the dynamo producing electricity, and religion is represented as the Virgin in Christianity. Religious beliefs, such as the miracles surrounding the Virgin, are a powerful motivational force. Similarly, beliefs in the power of technological invention and use can be a powerful force for human benefit and loss. Adams writes of himself in the third person: "...the dynamo itself was but an ingenious channel for conveying somewhere the heat latent in a few tons of poor coal hidden in a dirty engine-house...but to Adams the dynamo became a symbol of infinity... he began to feel the forty-foot dynamo as a moral force, much as the early Christians felt the Cross." Then, in describing the inspirational force behind great works of art, he writes, "...the force that created it all—the Virgin, the Woman—by whose genius the 'stately monuments of superstition' were built, through which she was expressed" (Adams, 1931, pp. 380, 387). In connecting beliefs and experience in the real world, Adams is careful to emphasize the nature and role of symbols. Worship, in the modern context, clearly distinguishes between the object, in this case fire, and whatever it represents.

An aside on technology and the time: Had Adams been aware of the latent power of geothermal heat under his perch on earth, he might have given his dynamo even greater leverage of power.

*Medicine*

"I swear by Apollo Physician and Asclepias and Hygieia and Panacea and all the gods and goddesses, making them my witnesses, that I will fulfill according to my ability and judgment this oath and this covenant..." (Hippocratic oath)[142]

Where might the relation between religion and human creation be more profound than in healing? Indeed, a great amount of the energy devoted to prayer and religious ritual has been, and still is, directed at curing some physiological or psychological affliction. At one extreme is "faith healing" wherein appeals to an invisible, magical force will, in itself, bring about a cure of some unwanted condition of body or mind. At another extreme would be uncritical, unquestioned reliance on the efficacy of prevailing medical aids and practices—perhaps another form of faith healing. Whatever level or form, the perceived relation between religion and health will influence the conduct of healer, afflicted, and community within which illness and healing happen. Religion can frame or limit medical practices and research.[143] It can influence perceptions of the cause, even the very nature, of a condition.

Galen of Pergamon (c. 130-200 CE), a physician as renowned as Hippocrates, made revolutionary contributions to physiology, including the relation between mental states and bodily conditions. He demonstrated experimentally the functions of the brain in relation to the network of nerves. He developed theories of behavior based on "animal spirits" carried in the fluid of tubes we call nerves. Other contributions were primal investigations of blood circulation, anticipating Harvey. In addition to his work in physiology, he had great interest in philosophy, basically Aristotelian, and the history and content of religion. He accepted the idea of natural law similar to that of the Stoics. Apparently, he accepted a universe created and guided by God to a degree amounting to determinism and much of the tenets of Christianity, but rejected the idea of miracles.

The career of Galen illustrates the span of connections and tensions of science, in his case physiology, and religion. Other Galileos, Darwins, and daVincis could add to the story of natural tension between belief and free inquiry. In medical practice and science, human intervention in nature's processes extends to life, health, and death of people and their fellow animals and plants. Whether intervening by appeal to invisible, magical forces or to the corporeal forces of scalpel, chemistry, or cell manipulation, the intent of meddling mankind is the same. What differs is just a matter of method. Science and religion are separate "Magisteria," to borrow a term from Stephen Jay Gould.[144] Both spheres are occupied by humans intending to intervene for the betterment of people or other beings. However, the actual, final effect of such intervention may or may not result in betterment of the individual, community, species, or planet. Think of the combined effect of the two Magisteria each pursuing its own ends. For example, medical science's success in reducing infant mortality, prolonging longevity, and enhancing fertility—combined with religious doctrines forbidding birth control— has exacerbated Earth's overpopulation.

## Organization Tools and God

"If money was not God, it appeared to be the next best thing."[145]

To the extent that human creations such as agriculture, fire management, and medicine intervene in natural processes, they could be said to be "playing God." The tools of organization–money, writing, and logic–are human creations, but nonetheless subject to oblations and prayers to a higher authority.

"In God We Trust" is pressed onto our currency. Its exchange is predicated on trust, that the symbol of value will be redeemable in kind. The first-order trust, then, is that the monetary system assures the holder that the coin, bill, or certificate of money will be honored in value when presented in exchange for a goat, bushel of wheat, laptop, or massage. God should enter only in last resort, after the bank's or sovereign's guarantee has failed. The slogan "In God We Trust" was injected into the American currency system by an Act of Congress in 1864, long after trust in money had presumably been established by government. Perhaps unseen forces guide the money system's functioning; if so, they are not always attentive to disruptive anomalies.

Money, a number-symbol of value, coupled with contracts in writing enlarged and revolutionized commerce. As money and writing transformed trade, they also changed arts, government, and cultures. Writing enabled history. Writing became power, in part through religion.

To the earliest illiterate masses, the first appearance of signs that could convey words without the presence of the author must have seemed miraculous. Even as writing became commonplace, the ability to write and read would be awesome and command authority. Moses descended the mountain with inscribed stone tablets, demonstrating the significance of *writing*, not reciting, the covenants.[146] The exact wording selected by Christian authorities to comprise the official, canonical word of God is paramount. Wrangling about semantics was so intense during his reign that James I of England commissioned a set of experts in 1611 to prepare a Bible that bore his name. Vast amounts of creative energy in monasteries, seminaries, and university departments have been devoted to scholastic research on religious text.

Writing technology made enormous differences in religious practices, and in the long run, the content and character of religions. Despite the existence of movable type in the Far East much earlier, the West awaited the Gutenberg press in 1440 to democratize literacy, mainly through the Gutenberg Bible (1455) and its successors. High-volume printing supported the emergence of the Renaissance and the Reformation of the Christian church. Today, most organized religions include a significant publishing arm.

Writing undoubtedly influenced the character and progress of systematic, critical thought. Writing helped to enforce discipline in the structure of reasoning and the storage of ideas for later review. Ideas that might be otherwise inaccessible could be communicated to others. Logic as we know it would have been impossible without writing.

Humans may be the only animal with concern about religion. Within the knowledge processes of detection, reflection, and correction, humans devote much of their attention and time to reflect upon (and sometimes correct) that which they are unable to detect. The faith aspect of religion offers explanations about the unknown. Faith is essentially a body of premises. And the rules of systematic reason—logic—are concerned with the validity of argument, independently of the reality of premises. No amount of logical precision will affirm or deny the truth of the premises.

Yet the importance that humans attach to the relation between reason or logic and religion is emphasized by the existence of a whole subdiscipline of philosophy labeled "the philosophy of religion." *The Oxford Companion to Philosophy* describes the philosophy of religion as "...typically includ[ing] the rationality of belief in God, the demonstrability of God's existence, the logical character of religious language, and apparent contradictions between divine attributes and the features of the world—say, between omnipotence and evil..." (p. 759).

In his book, *The Logic of Religion,* Jude Dougherty states that a philosophical analysis of religion begins with the assent to certain propositions, i.e., there is a God. That assent is "a more-or-less gratuitous act of faith." Faith in the proposition is "acknowledged to be true but for which there is no evidence, scientific or otherwise" (Dougherty, 2003, p. 9). Dougherty's book examines ruminations on religion by renowned classic and modern (mostly Western) philosophers. At the end of his book, Dougherty observes that "... although its object be God, religion is a human invention subject to all the vagaries which characterize human endeavor" (p. 167). Logic can arrange propositions so that they are valid, hence consistent or reasonable, yet add nothing to the reality-truth of the propositions or to conclusion of the argument.

The idea of reason or logic need not be set against the idea of God. Indeed, the oft-cited New Testament passage that opens the book of John merges the two ideas:

"In the beginning was the Word (Logos), and the Word (Logos) was with God, and the Word (Logos) was God."

The passage appears to be a direct declaration on the relation of reason (logos) and God. And it calls for description—a clear, unambiguous definition—of God.[147] However, neither the passage nor the remainder of John appear to provide such a definition, or at least not a definition accessible to the average reader. What the passage does suggest is that God is of the mind, that is, reason manifest in word(s). Any useful or meaningful argument involving God would seem to call for definitions in the words of premises, and that implies a proposition such as "God is...."[148]

But how important is the God definition to human outlook and/or behavior? The Abrahamic religions, for example, stress good and evil as cosmic forces influencing ethical principles and a moral code to guide behavior. A focal force seems necessary to define and judge behavior. Buddhism contains ethical principles and a moral code heavily based on reason and reflection, but without addressing ultimate forces and creation origins. Buddhism is sometimes listed among religions, but not considered a religion. Likewise, Stoicism stresses a moral code and behavior without great concern about creation or God, and although Christianity draws heavily on Stoic concepts and ideas, Stoicism is called a philosophy and is not listed among religions.

Clearly, the efficacy of any conclusions from an argument about the relation between reason and God will depend critically on the definition (concept) of God. Philosophically, this is heavy stuff. Stephen Jay Gould recommends hands off as the best approach with his idea of NOMA, Non-Overlapping Magisteria, the separation of church and science (Gould 1999). Another approach is <u>As If.</u>

## As If

The ultimate test of a good model is its ability to explain and predict, or in other terms, account for. The settling quality of predictability has a psychological benefit and provides practical, day-to-day, solutions. The "As If" model claims no abstract reality or ultimate truth—it claims only that it works. If, for example, a proper planting time can be prescribed by observing planet locations in a Ptolemaic universe, and the strategy continues to produce good crops, it can be used by farmers long after Copernicus and Galileo posit a more realistic universe. The wise farmer says "I will plant <u>as if</u> Ptolemy were telling me when. I see the sun coming up in the east, a little sooner every day in the spring. Sun appears <u>as if</u> swinging around the earth. Good enough."

Economists employ abstract mathematical models to state generalities about human behavior. Milton Friedman, for example, explains that economic hypotheses "...behave in the world of observation *as if* they occurred in a hypothetical and highly simplified world containing only the forces that the hypothesis asserts to be important" and that "...businessmen do not actually and literally solve the system of simultaneous equations in terms of which the mathematical economist finds it convenient to express this hypothesis..."[149] Hans Vaihinger developed a formal expression of the "as if" philosophy in the early 20th century.[150] He was anticipated by Jeremy Bentham's *The Theory of Fictions* in the 18th century.[151]

Bentham's interest in the power, use, and misuse of symbols came into focus soon after his entry to Oxford, 1760, at age 12. At 16, from attending Blackstone's lectures he developed his critique of legal fictions: "...a Fiction of Law may be defined in general as the saying something exists which does not exist, and acting as if it existed; or *vice versa.*"[152] Bentham's critique of legal fictions was extended to language generally and to the great mischiefs inherent in "Word-magic." From wariness about abuses of fictions, however, he acknowledges the functions of fictions in human transactions. Thus, fictions can contribute to greater happiness.[153]

Vaihinger (1852-1933) opens his book, *The Philosophy of As If,* with an autobiographical chapter relating his growing up in a religious atmosphere and early studies touching on philosophic and theologic ideas. He developed a strong interest in the history of mankind. He wrote: "The idea of evolution became one of the fundamental elements of my mental outlook."[154] From "...Plato's myths [in *Republic*] the seed was sown...which later I myself named the "World of 'As If'." He wrote that Kant was particularly important in his philosophical orientation: "...from his doctrine that action, the practical, must take the first place...supremacy of practical reason." Vaihinger's notion of fictions makes much of a distinction between "as-if" and "hypothesis," the former being consciously false and the latter being provisional, i.e., open to revision. On this distinction, he is mildly critical of Adam Smith's economic fiction and Bentham's political fiction.[155]

On religion, as in many other matters, Vaihinger draws on Kant who he cites as saying, "God is not a substance outside of me but merely a moral relation within me...the categorical imperative does not assume a substance issuing its commands from on high...but is a commandment or a prohibition of my own reason."[156] Kant's views were extended in the work of Friedrich Karl Forberg, whom Vaihinger claims makes the clearest statements on the religion of As-if. He says that religion is not a matter of indifference about what we do. It is a duty (think moral imperative). And further, "...it is not a duty to believe that there exists a moral world-government or a God as a moral world -ruler; our duty is simply to act *as if* we believed it."[157]

"As-ifs" are fictions put to work and so have a distinct scent of pragmatism. The "As-if" fiction makes no claim to reality, or even offer a route to test reality. Its utility rests on performance. In the history of mankind, the idea of God appears to have been a powerful organizing force. Has that idea required a definitive test of reality? No. Despite a seemingly endless rhetoric on the existence or non-existence of God, the practical goods or ills from the idea carry on. As a human creation, God serves as an explanation for the unexplained, a repository of mystery, a holding-pen for challenges to knowledge. Those accepting such challenges may employ NOMA, "As-ifs" or perhaps some other mode.

Other working fictions are metaphors, allegories, fables, myths, sagas, and such. Like "as-ifs," they are tools. Some fictions are tools to reveal another, perhaps deeper, reality. Some fictions simply entertain, inspire, or console. The risk of fictions is failure to recognize them as such, and impede mankind's survival mechanism of detection, reflection, and correction. Consider fiction's comfort of illusion. Faced with the worst of times, even when brought on by one's foolishness or vanity, one may enlist fantasy to avoid unpleasantness. Consider the lines from Shakespeare's King Lear,[158] who comforts Cordelia as they set off to their doom in prison:

"...let's away to prison:
We two alone will sing like birds i' the cage:
When thou dost ask me blessing, I'll kneel down
And ask of thee forgiveness: so we'll live,
And pray, and sing, and tell old tales, and laugh
At gilded butterflies..."[159]

## A Godly Sum

Creations are accumulations of knowledge with new concepts, discoveries, and inventions. When the volume in the sphere of knowledge expands, the mysteries, puzzlements, and unknowns expand like the surface of that sphere. The good news is that God supplies solace and security in the face of the unknown. The bad news is that solace and security can preclude curiosity and invention, the engines of creation.

A principal theme throughout this essay is that mankind's expanded and expanding knowledge does not diminish the unknown but, indeed, expands the unknown, the theater for fictions, and imaginative explanations for the unexplained. The "as-if" fictions can be useful, even powerful, but when no longer productive, they should find their place in history.

From the as-if perspective, then, the existence of God is simply viewed pragmatically—that is, if it is useful, use it; if not, don't. God as a fiction can be a tool in morals management. In the morals management role, God is an everpresent observer, judge, and administrator of rewards and punishments. For those responsive to rewards for "rights" and punishments for "wrongs," the God model can be an effective tool.[160]  On the other hand, for the pure deontologist whose decisions are based solely on doing right just because it's right and refraining from wrong because it's wrong, the God model may be superfluous.  There are arguments for God other than morals management, such as respecting and honoring the power of the unknown.  And then, possibly most important, the God model may provide a basis for human creativity.

# Afterword

The U.S. Bureau of Census projects the population of the United States to be 458 million and of the world to be 9.3 billion by 2050. From 2010, in years representing only half a typical American's lifespan, the United States will add more than 140 million people and the world 2.3 billion. By comparison, it took the entire habitation of Homo sapiens on earth up to 1950 to rise to a number equaling the forthcoming 40-year increase.

So how many human beings are optimal to maintain the well-being of people and their nations or planet? The question festers, but seems not to breach the forums of human discourse. When population issues are addressed at all, they are couched in terms of coping with agricultural, energy, medical, organizational, and other concerns. Yet virtually all these concerns arise from, or are exacerbated by, growth in population. The creative genius that underlies agriculture and medicine seems mute in addressing the population question. Humans, claiming earthly domination as their birthright, seem unable or unwilling to control themselves.

Environmentalists appear to have limitless energy for studying and dispensing advice on behavior that best advances conservation, in the interests of preserving the planet. The message inherent in *Seven Creations* supports, or is at least consistent with, this environmentalist view, i.e, to ensure their well-being and that of the planet that supports them, people must become *smarter, stronger,* and *smaller. Smarter* as in an enlarged capacity to acquire and use knowledge; *stronger* as in more durable without resorting to medicinal or surgical advances; *smaller* as in less burdensome on the resources required for life and living.

But smarter, stronger, and smaller are not enough. People must be fewer. Even the best conceived policies to promote environmental behavior, bolster productivity, or improve health can be swamped by the pressures of sheer numbers, knowledge deficiencies, or geographic inequities. Lack of self-control will lead to self-destruction.

The *Seven Creations* honors the brain's capacity to achieve human survival. Indeed, it is the human brain that has allowed a relatively weak, slow, and insensate species to survive and prosper. That brain (aided by prehensile thumbs) extended the creative processes by adaptations, by *detection, reflection,* and *correction.* Consensus on corrective population policies at all levels—global to personal—surely must be possible.

Accumulating knowledge enlarges understanding and simultaneously stokes awareness of new areas of ignorance and mystery. These new uncertainties—both cosmological and corporeal— engage the curiosity of science and challenge the tenets of religious faith. Human creativity is, as Merwin would say, more than survival, but life itself.

# Endnotes

[1] (Merwin 2005, p.121) Note: he uses no punctuation marks—
only lines and capital letters.

[2] Incidental domestication simply reflects the relationship
between humans and the plants on which they feed; people
will favor, consume, and spread certain plants even as they are
found in the environment. Specialized domestication involves
awareness and intentional protection of preferred plants and
destruction of competitors. Agricultural domestication is the
purposeful manipulation of the environment for favored seeds
and plants through weeding, fertilizing, watering, and other
protective practices (Rindos, 1984, pp. 153-166).

[3] Somewhere in their evolution, sheep and goats may have
had some common ancestry (Buckland, 1983, pp. 1349-59).
However, for the period here defined as agriculture, they remain
distinct species, *Ovis aries* and *Capra hircus,* respectively.

[4] According to Kujit and Finlayson (2009), storage of wild grass
seeds preceded the cultivation of domestic grains by at least a
millennium. Still the "origin" of agriculture is perhaps best
dated with domestication.

[5] However, as Rindos (1984) points out, settlement and agriculture are not necessarily pre-conditions, one for the other:

"...full sedentism has apparently preceded developed agricultural systems in certain parts of the world, whereas in other places agricultural systems have become well established long before the advent of settled village life" (p.173).

6   Early in the 19th century, scientists identified the chemical salicin, extracted from willow plants, useful for relieving pain. The chemical was refined, synthesized, and buffered to become aspirin. And from an extract of the Pacific Yew collected by the U.S. Department of Agriculture in 1962, scientists developed a treatment for breast cancer. Later, the compound was found in the more common English Yew, and work continues to synthesize the chemicals. Other plants—like the opium poppy and marijuana—have medicinal as well as recreational uses.

7   Genetic modification greatly accelerates the customization of plants and animals, including people, to achieve desired characteristics. From earlier DNA work by Watson, Crick, and others, genetic engineering of plants, animals, bacteria, yeasts, insects, and the like developed in the 1960s and continues as a major industry. Farmers, for example, regularly plant seeds engineered to resist the toxic substances used to kill weeds. Scientists in the 1980s genetically engineered bacteria to produce insulin. In 1985, the U.S. National Institutes of Health approved the study of the treatment of human defects with engineered genes.

8   Common bread wheat is a hexaploid carrying three times the chromosomes as the diploid einkorn. Durum and emmer are tetraploids, with twice the chromosomes of einkorn. Because some people are allergic to bread wheat gluten, research is exploring the potential of einkorn and emmer for breadmaking.

9   Nesbitt (2001) finds that bread wheat's ancestors, einkorn and emmer, were domesticated as early as 10,000 BP (7500 BCE, uncalibrated). His article helps to explain much of the variation

and uncertainty about wheat's early years of plant evolution and the transition from foraging to farming.

[10] The overbearing importance of corn is the thesis of Michael Pollan's *Omnivore's Dilemma* (2007). The dominance of this plant and its commerce in the life and diet of the consumer vividly portrays domestication gone wrong, or at least rogue.

[11] The heading is drawn from biblical Matthew 4:4 and Deuteronomy 8:3, whose context is considerably broader than agriculture or food and fiber. However, the words do serve as reminder that agricultural interventions in nature apply to more than food.

[12] One of the grisly features of American history is the massive slaughter of the bison solely for pelts, the remains of carcasses left to rot. The twin objectives of the slaughter were profits for the buffalo hunters and tradesmen, and destruction of a principal source of livelihood of Native Americans to bring them into submission. Another view is that of Martin Garretson: "No intelligent excuse can be offered for the senseless slaughter and awful waste of a valuable and harmless animal purely for personal gain or to satisfy a blood-lust to kill" (Quote from David Dary. 1974, p. 69).

[13] The International Council of Tanners reports that the leather industry produces about 18 billion square feet of leather per year. The Council, citing FAO statistics, states that international trade of leather is "much bigger than meat and other commonly recognized commodities."

[14] Dating of the origins of weaving is controversial. Imprints on clay of fabrics and weaving suggest dates as far back as 27,000 years ago. Jacquard weaving, patented in 1801, produced an exceptionally fine cloth on a loom employing punch cards, which were the forerunner of modern computers.

[15] James I, when not busy governing his nation and directing the composition of a new scholarly version of the Christian Bible,

was attempting to establish (unsuccessfully) a silk industry in England.

[16]  U.S. Department of Agriculture, Foreign Agricultural Service, May 2010.

[17]  Harlan, 1995, p.219.

[18]  Miller and Gleason, 1994, p. 33.

[19]  Oxen also supplied, and in places still do, work power in agriculture and transportation. However, the horse with a fitted collar can provide 50% more foot-pounds per second because of the horse's greater speed and endurance.

[20]  Credit for the modern steam engine is often assigned to James Watt in the mid-18th century, although rudimentary engines date much earlier. Watt-type engines featured in the development of the railroads.

[21]  Although rooted in earlier systematic thought, Aristotelian logic exemplifies the ordered thinking needed for later developments in science. Roger Bacon and 13th century contemporaries blended reason and empirical verification to provide a basis for modern science. This was one more step in the evolution of human domination of natural forces.

[22]  U.S. Department of Agriculture, May 15; The Homestead Act, May 20; Morrill Land Grant College Act, July 2, all 1862 (Rasmussen, 1960).

[23]  The role and accomplishments of the Department of Agriculture are summarized in *Century of Service: The First 100 years of the United States Department of Agriculture* (USDA, 1963).

[24]  The story of the green revolution is artfully incorporated in a biography of Norman Borlaug written by Leon Hesser (2006).

[25]  In 1998, a new strain of stem rust was indentified in Africa, and has since spread to other countries. The new rust strain could threaten the world's food supply if resistant wheat is not developed quickly. Borlaug's methodical approach is now too slow to prevent a worldwide food catastrophe. The stem rust

challenge dramatically illustrates the need for research and education to support agriculture.

26 This assumes that *Homo sapiens*, modern humans, emerged out of hominid evolution 150,000 to 200,000 years ago (Lockwood, 2007, p. 101) and that the population was approximately 2,000, according to Wikipedia, *World Population*, Estimated world population at various dates, 70,000 BCE.

27 Estimates vary. The figure used is from U.S. Census Bureau historical estimates (Census, 2008).

28 For examples, note Bangladesh 366 per sq mi; Australia, 0.96 per sq mi; and United States, 11.6 per sq mi.

29 Some additional land is recoverable from other uses such as forest. In Mato Grosso, Brazil, vast areas of highly productive agriculture have been carved from the Amazon rainforest, much of it illegally but without serious prohibition. Such shifts in resource use can have negative long-term effects on the balance of life forms on the planet, but are nonetheless profitable to individuals in the short run.

30 Figures are from National Geographic website Environment "Freshwater," 2010. For more on the water problem growing out of agriculture's thirst, read William Ashworth's *Ogallala Blue: Water and Life on the High Plains.*

31 In the beginning of Mumford's venerable *The City in History,* he acknowledges the importance of agriculture in settlement and eventually the city, but stands the relationship on its head. His argument seems to be that the village settlement brought forth agriculture, rather than agriculture being the force that enabled settlement, thence cities. Referring to permanent settlements from India to the Baltic Sea: "With these Mesolithic hamlets come the first clearings for agricultural purposes; likewise the earliest domesticated animals....Thus the very act of settlement in villages helped to make agriculture self-sustaining" (Mumford, 1961, pp. 10,14). Perhaps it is a chicken-egg argument.

But few would dispute agriculture's support of the existence and growth of cities.

[32] City statistics depend not only on the timing of the count but also the boundaries. Some data are for a prescribed legal entity, others for a metropolitan area variously defined. Suffice here to say there are many very large agglomerations of people that depend on distant sources of food and fiber. Data here are from World Atlas.com, in turn taken from the U.S. Census Bureau and *Times Atlas of the World*.

[33] Cantillon's *Essai sur la Nature du Commerce en General* was published in 1755 and became one of the underpinnings of the school of economists known as the physiocrats. The *Essai* was also a source for Malthus.

[34] Wilson's (2006) book is a scientific argument addressed to an unnamed Southern Baptist pastor, seeking an alliance of faith and reason to preserve the Earth's diversity of life. The argument is dominated by *diversity* of species, but he also recognizes the importance of *reducing human numbers*: "With the smaller population [of humans] that can be reached within the century, and a higher and sustainable per capita consumption spread more evenly around the world, this planet can be paradise" (p. 90).

[35] Philosopher Paul Thompson argues that traditional environmental ethics inadequately account for agriculture's necessary food producing function and further neglect the farmers' role as natural stewards of the land in which "...good farming has been expressed in terms of care for the soil, water, plants, and animals under the farmer's supervision" (Thompson,1995, p. 72).

[36] A neat summation of the issue is contained in reviews by Helen Epstein in the *New York Review of Books* (vol. 55, no. 13, August 14, 2008) of Matthew Connelly's *Fatal Misconception: The Struggle to Control World Population,* and M. Catherine

Maternowska's *Reproducing Inequities: Poverty and the Politics of Population in Haiti.*

[37] In simplest terms, the calories needed to sustain a person are directly proportional to the person's weight. For example, a moderately active 200-pound person requires about 3,100 calories, approximately twice that of a moderately active 100-pound person. The relationship holds for all levels of activity and all weight comparisons (see Harvard Medical School, *Heart Healthy Eating Made Simple,* p. 15). The message to agriculture is that the burden of producing food for a population of 200-pounders is twice that of the same number of 100-pounders.

[38] Contained in Schumacher's landmark *Small is Beautiful: Economics as if People Mattered.*

[39] The announcement was made in *Science,* May 20, 2010, from the Craig Venter Institute in summary form: "Creation of a Bacterial Cell Controlled by a Chemically Synthesized Genome." The announcement in a context briefing on artificial life forms is discussed lucidly in *The Economist* magazine, May 22, 2010, pp. 81-83.

[40] Recall that CAFO is defined as "confined animal feeding operation." Large- scale agriculture, representing only 12 percent of farms in the U.S., provides more than 84 percent of the value of agricultural production. The small family farms responsible for 16 percent of the value of production hold 63 percent of farm assets and 64 percent of agricultural land. All size classes of farms get income from non-agricultural sources, but many small farms have net earnings from agriculture of zero—or less. The household income from off-farm activity for all farms, large and small combined, is 86 percent; for large farms this averages about 14 percent, and for some classes of small farms off-farm income accounts for more than 100 percent of total income. That is, some small farms actually lose money farming, but

make it up from pension, investment, or nonfarm employment (Hoppe et al., 2010).

[41] Several sources credit Newcomen with the first application of steam principles that had been understood for centuries, but only as a curiosity. Newcomen brought forth his engine in 1712 to pump water from mine shafts. In 1769, Watt patented a steam engine that was basically an improvement on the Newcomen design and a prototype for the steam engine. A steam turbine engine to generate electricity was patented by Parsons in 1884. For agriculture, the application of steam power to railroad locomotives probably was of greater significance than field traction because steam tractors were large, clumsy, and soon replaced by gasoline and diesel farm tractors. The end of the 19th century saw the apex in horse-drawn mechanization. The beginning of the 20th century saw the shift to gasoline- and diesel-driven equipment that continues today.

[42] To the extent that fuel production competes with food, using agricultural products for fuel is controversial.

[43] A basic treatment of the nature of fire, thorough but non-technical, is found in a U.S. Army technical manual, *Firefighting and Rescue Procedures,* TM 5-315, 1971, chapter 3: "The Characteristics, Chemistry, and Physics of Fire." For more sophisticated treatments of fire, see the *Combustion and Flame* journal.

[44] A helpful chronology of metal is included in Alan Cramb's *A Short History of Metals.* He notes that, of the 86 metals known today, only 7 had been discovered/used before the 16th century.

[45] Bronze can be an alloy of copper and other metals such as zinc (called brass) and aluminum.

[46] The pressure to adopt iron was due not only to its own qualities but to the scarcity of tin to make bronze.

[47] See, for example, Jared Diamond's (1997) account of the Spanish invasion of the New World.

48    Chinese alchemists as early as the 2nd century BCE discovered the explosive qualities of a combination of charcoal, saltpeter, and sulfur, which was further developed into the 13th and 14th centuries CE to produce an explosive. Franciscan Roger Bacon of Oxford, for example, published a charcoal formula for black gunpowder in 1242 CE, which became the weapon standard until nitroglycerin-based explosives and propellants in the 18th century CE. Developers of the latter included Alfred Nobel, who invented the nitro variation ballistite in 1887.

49    The use of coal, even for domestic purposes, is relatively recent. In Britain, for example, the Roman occupiers (1st to 5th centuries) were aware of coal's flammability, but its use for household heating and blacksmithing awaited the 13th and 14th centuries.

50    Obsidian also may be a suitable material for contemporary surgical scalpels. Buck (1982) comments that "ancient man in several areas of the world had access to cutting blades of volcanic glass which were sharper than the surgical instruments of today" (p. 269).

51    Empedocles (c. 495-35 BC) was a pre-Socratic philosopher noted for his metaphysics, in which he specified the four elements of nature to be water, air, fire, and earth (Kirk, 1983, p. 286).

52    Over 85 percent of U.S. energy is from fossil fuels, with petroleum accounting for 39 percent, natural gas 23 percent, and coal 23 percent . (U.S. Dept.Energy, EIA, 2007)

53    Enhanced oil recovery techniques were developed relatively recently, in the early 1940s (Lake et al., 1992, p. 56), as the economics of oil recovery made it profitable. Previously, oil wells were simply shut down when recovery became too expensive, often with less than 25 percent of the oil recovered.

54    Radiation from the sun warms the surface of Earth's crust, which stores heat at shallow depths. This heat can be

transferred to warm water, circulated by heat pumps, for heating and cooling living and working spaces.

[55] Current HDR techniques applied in some areas may cool the hot rocks to a point of uneconomic use in 20 to 30 years, requiring the relocation of extraction and/or generation.

[56] An exajoule is $10^{18}$ joules. A joule is a measure of energy or force; in practical terms, it is approximately the energy needed to lift a small apple 1 meter. A joule is also the energy required to produce 1 watt of electricity for 1 second. Thus, a kilowatt hour equals 3,600,000 joules.

[57] British thermal units, BTUs, are a measure of energy to incorporate all sources. Primary energy flow in the U.S. from all sources was 94.6 Quadrillion BTUs in 2009. (U.S. EIA August 2010 AER) of which 78.4 were oil, gas, and coal, and 8,3 were nuclear, 7.7 were renewable (hydro, geothermal, solar, wind, biomass).

[58] Much of the remaining capacity—about 30,000 MW—is from low-head/low-power sources (see Idaho National Laboratory: http://hydro2.inel.gov/resourceassessment/index.shtml).

[59] Rivetna, 2002, p. 37.

[60] Some scholars think that they are two parts of the same poem.

[61] Earlier treatises on medical diagnoses and treatments date to 1600 BCE and before in Mesopotamia, Iran, and far Eastern regions. While acknowledging the contributions of Egyptian, Mesopotamian, Indian, and Chinese medicine, the evolution of medicine here begins with early Greek and Roman settings to illustrate the course of human intervention in the natural processes of damage and disease of people.

[62] Greeks and others carried much of their knowledge about medicine to Rome, but contributions by Rome itself were not distinguished. However, Rome's great contribution to public health was the development of waterworks and sewerage systems.

63  The significance of blood in life is abundantly asserted in biblical writings, like Leviticus 16.

64  Note later in the Money chapter reference to "animal spirits" borrowed from Galen by Keynes and later by Akerloff and Shiller.

65  Named from the German physician Alois Alzheimer who, in 1906, first identified the debilitating and finally fatal brain disease.

66  The prairie dog is a known host to the Plague fleas, which accounted for two American deaths as recently as 1996.

67  The term "vaccinate" is derived from *vaca*, Latin for cow.

68  Poliomyelitis is a highly infectious virus that occurs in three strains, with consequences ranging from no apparent effect to death or serious muscular disability. During the 1950s, Salk and Sabin vaccines were developed to control all three strains. Vaccination, particularly among children, has been successful in controlling the disease.

69  A framework of war as a disease might begin with Boulding's classic *Conflict and Defense: A General Theory* (1962). He opens with: "Conflict is an activity that is found almost everywhere. It is found throughout the biological world, where the conflict both of individuals and of species is an important part of the picture." Disease is a conflict between pathogen and subject. The conflict is within subjects, and as an epidemic, a community of subjects. Medicine is an ally of human subjects, and their chosen other species.

70  A modern-day illustration of relief from mysticism was announced by a doctors' panel appointed by the Catholic Church in 1954 to examine the healings claimed for Lourdes. The panel reported in 2008 that henceforth doctors' evaluations of healings at Lourdes would be limited to "remarkable," not "miraculous."

71    Using BioBrick© standard biological parts, a synthetic biologist or biological engineer can already, to some extent, program living organisms in the same way a computer scientist can program a computer. The DNA sequence information and other characteristics of BioBrick© standard biological parts are made available to the public free of charge currently via MIT's Registry of Standard Biological Parts. Underway is a growing industry of creating biological parts available for reassembly in designer combinations, much like standardized automotive parts, e.g., spark plugs, tires, batteries.

72    Usher, drawing on guesstimates of several anthropologists, cited life expectancy of hunter-gatherers preceding and into the agricultural era at 31.4 years, with life expectancies in some areas—e.g., England-Wales 1348-75 (Black Death)—as brief as 17.3 years. All such estimates are based on unrecorded archaeological evidence and assumptions, but mass extinctions took place before relatively recent times, and could occur again.

73    In 2010, British biologist Robert Edwards won a Nobel Prize for his research on in vitro fertilization, leading to a clinical treatment for infertility. The procedure opens the door to cloning and characteristic selection such as for sex, coloration, size, or any other desired feature. It also enables members of the species with a fertility disability to carry the DNA of that disability forward to successive generations via human intervention. (In nature, this disability would die out.) Thus, in vitro fertilization, under some conditions, could render the reproductive process entirely dependent on clinical intervention.

74    Nature and one of its offspring, *homo sapiens,* have been engaged in a struggle for dominance, and in the story written by that offspring its successes have been deemed progress. Bronowski (1973) even labeled it the *The Ascent of Man.* The struggle is interesting. Humans are no match for nature by any physical measure. Other of nature's creatures can better see, smell,

run, hear, resist heat or cold, reproduce, endure, adapt, etc. Brainpower has allowed humans to compete with nature via a form of jiu-jitsu, using nature's own power to serve human ends. However, the story is not finished. It remains to be seen how the struggle will end, by whom the story will be told, and whether it will be labeled "progress." Incidentally, in his history of finance, *The Ascent of Money,* Niall Ferguson credits Bronowski for his title inspiration.

[75] D. Foley's entry, "Money," appears in Eatwell et al., 1987. *The New Palgrave Dictionary of Economics*, NY: Stockton Press, vol. 3, pp. 519-525. A matching entry on money by James Tobin appears in the revised *New Palgrave*, 2008.

[76] Adam Smith opens his chapter on the origin and use of money in *Wealth of Nations* this way: "When the division of labor has been once thoroughly established, it is but a very small part of a man's wants which the produce of his own labor can supply. He supplies the far greater part of them by exchanging that surplus part of the produce of his own labor which is over and above his own consumption, for such parts of the produce of other men's labor as he has occasion for. Every man thus lives by exchanging, or becomes in some measure a merchant, and the society itself grows to be what is properly a commercial society" (Smith {1776} 1937, p. 22).

[77] Smith tells the same story in cattle and salt exchange, then leads into metals "above every other commodity." He takes into account frauds and abuses, requiring all countries to "affix a public stamp upon certain quantities of such particular metals" (Smith {1776} 1937, p. 25).

[78] For full discussion of bible time money, see Harper's Bible Dictionary... "Money."

[79] Although, with a stretch, it is possible to argue the origins of banking much earlier, the manipulation and management of money in modern times began when communication and

documentation enabled accounts, and legal facilities for large, complex transactions. A fuller, more studious trace of the origins of banking would include the temple moneychangers, the abundant stores of wealth in houses of worship, money for the crusades, the impact of foreign exploration and conquest, and the branch banking of Genoese institutions throughout Europe in Medieval times. Galbraith, by contrast, took as his beginning of banking the formation of the Bank of England in 1694—*The Bank* (Galbraith, 1975, pp. 28-44).

[80] The creation of currency in America has not always been under central or even state control. In the 1837-1863 era, for example, there was no central bank. In some periods individual banks, numbering as many as 30,000, made their own notes whose value fluctuated wildly and hastened bank failure. The National Bank Act of 1863, revised in 1864-6, established the system of nationally chartered banks and stipulated a nationally uniform currency.

[81] Government securities in the form of bills, bonds, and notes are similar to liens on property or promissory notes in the private sector. The "security" is based on government's ability to tax, rentals of government property, and fees/charges for some government services or access to places. Taxes (notably individual income and social insurance, at about 80 percent of Federal revenue) represent the principal sources of financial wealth of the Federal Government.

[82] Akerlof and Shiller (2009) have blown fresh air on the coals of an old philosophical debate/distinction between rational and intuitive brain work. They revived, developed, and even titled their book *Animal Spirits*, a term tossed off by Keynes (Keynes, 1961 [1936], pp. 161-2) in his explanation for behavior affecting herd responses to economic events. Thus, Akerlof and Shiller free economics from having to define and model the state of an economy in terms only of reasoned, calculating

behavior of the economy's members. Irrational exuberance is instead non-rational exuberance, that is, just not in the rational/irrational frame at all. A much earlier source of the idea of "animal spirits" is attributed to Galen (c. 200 CE), who developed the hypothesis of "animal spirits" that flowed as invisible fluid in nerves imagined as hollow tubes. This precursor to the concept of a nervous system in human physiology helped lay the groundwork for modern medicine's connections between brain and behavior.

[83]  For reasons more complex than simple convenience, however, the Euro was created to include a geographic community of nations. The American dollar and some other currencies such as the Swiss franc and the Australian dollar are recognized as, or are tied to, the currency of other nations. As yet there is no single international currency, although such a possibility has been discussed. Within each nation, one currency is used for exchanges, stores of value, and measures of account. In the United States, the supply of money is defined in three measures, M1, M2, and M3. Simply stated, M1 is the currency—bills and coins—plus deposits in checking accounts and travelers' checks; M2 is all of M1 plus savings accounts, time deposits of less than $100,000, and money market accounts; M3 is M1 + M2 plus other large time deposits, money market funds, and financial instruments. The M3 is a mystery money supply, unknown to the general public.

[84]  Robert Shiller writes on "a unit of account," meaning that prices are quoted in money units. He extends the unit of account idea with an index to some generally agreed standard such as the consumer price index. He notes that Chile has such an indexed unit of account (UF) in addition to the peso (Shiller, 1998, p. 2 *passim*).

[85]  Schumpeter emphasized the dynamic quality of a capitalist economy (principle would apply to any economy) in his

chapter on the process of creative destruction: "The essential point to grasp is that in dealing with capitalism we dealing with an evolutionary process...Capitalism, then, is by nature a form or method of economic change and not only never is, but never can be, stationary" (Schumpeter, 1976, p. 82).

[86]   In the sense Schumacher meant by "economics as if people mattered" (Schumacher, 1973).

[87]   Not to imply that money is beyond comprehension. Galbraith said of the money idea: "There is nothing about money that cannot be understood by the person of reasonable curiosity, diligence and intelligence" (Galbraith, 1975, p. 5).

[88]   Because of money's critical role in the economy's functions, it is an instrument of power wielded unfortunately by some concerned with their own, and not society's, well-being. Robert Wilmer, for example, wrote in the *Washington Post* (July 27, 2009) that the financial crisis of the time was due to financial organizations operating outside of the traditional banking system without the "safety and soundness that apply to banks and without obligation to make clear the extent of such firm's debt, leverage, capital or reserves."

[89]   Durant, 1953, p. 71.

[90]   Leakey and Lewin summarized human origins: "We are creatures of knowledge, it is true. But, more important, we are creatures driven to know" (Leakey, 1992, p. 33); or Toynbee: "...the event which dates the first appearance of human nature in the biosphere is neither the development of an anatomical feature nor the acquisition of an accomplishment; the historic event is Man's awakening to consciousness" (Toynbee, 1976, p. 23). And Young noted that, in the evolution of the human brain, tool making and using preceded philosophy: "Perhaps one of the most important influences in improving the perceptual powers of early man was his manipulation of objects..." (Young, 1971, p. 486).

91  See King and Shapiro, 1995, "Logic, History of," in T. Honderich, *The Oxford Companion to Philosophy,* NY: Oxford University Press, for a compressed history of Western logic from Aristotle to modern mathematical systems. However, the casual reader might be challenged by King and Shapiro and may, instead, enjoy the logic parts of Bertrand Russell's *History of Western Philosophy* or Will Durant's *The Story of Philosophy,* in which he slyly deflates Aristotle: "He [Aristotle] thinks the syllogism a description of man's way of reasoning, whereas it merely describes man's way of dressing up his reasoning for the persuasion of another mind..." But then Durant follows with: "Aristotle's creation of this new discipline of thought, and his firm establishment of its essential lines, remain among the lasting achievements of the human mind" (Durant, 1953, p. 71).

92  The AEIO statements placed in opposition to one another form a "square of opposition." From the square of opposition, Copi explains: "Given the truth or falsehood of any one of the four standard form categorical propositions, the truth or falsehood of some or all of the others can be inferred immediately" (Copi, 1986 p. 180). For examples: A being true, E is false, I is true, O is false; and I being false, A is false, E is true, O is true; but I being true, E is false, A is undetermined, O is undetermined. Similar interpretations of the elements examined here can be found in other, and more recent, introductions to logic. Recent publications are cited, along with an excellent online exposition of the categorical syllogism (http://philosophypages.com/lg/e08a.htm) by Garth Kemerling.

93  The middle term connects the premises: 1 = S of major, P of minor; 2 = P of major and minor; 3 = S of major and minor; 4 = P of major, S of minor. The middle term is never in the conclusion of a valid argument.

94 The statements shown here are rudimentary, simple. Statements may compound, or statements may not be explicit, their content merely implied—called enthymemes.

95 Venn diagrams are sets of overlapping circles to show inclusiveness/exclusiveness of terms in premises, from which can be shown the conclusion. They are named for John Venn, 19th century English logician/theoretical statistician.

96 Aristotle and his predecessors devised the Law of the Excluded Middle, which states that every proposition must either be true or false. Grass is either green or not green; it clearly cannot be both green and not green. But not everyone agreed, and Plato indicated there was a third region, beyond true and false, where these opposites "tumbled about."

97 Archeological evidence indicates that awareness of classes, units, time, and even perhaps arithmetic extends to as much as 70 millennia BP, but historical evidence such as recorded in Egyptian glyphs corresponds roughly to the creation of writing, before the 3rd millennium BCE.

98 Some numbers have taken on an iconic, even religious, quality. For example, phi, "the divine proportion" (1.618....), is thought to have particular aesthetic power, from anatomy to architecture. The number 20 is the standard of vision, i.e., 20/20 regarded as perfect sight. The biblical 12 is a symbol of perfection, as is 7, which also implies completeness.

99 Bell attributes to Gauss the crowning of arithmetic as "the Queen of Mathematics" (Newman, 1956, p. 498).

100 Practical applications of the compound interest idea include the simple "Rule of 72," which approximates the number of iterations, or years, it takes for an amount to double in size. For example, the years it takes the value of a $100 investment to become $200, at 6 percent interest per year, is 72/6 = 12.

101 The dating of the origin of *homo sapiens* varies widely, ranging from 150,000 to 200,000 years or more.

[102] Population Reference Bureau. 2010. *World Population Data Sheet.* Washington, DC. Reported total of 6.89 billion, growing at the rate of 158 per minute (number of births minus deaths).

[103] Early Egyptian geometry was devised as an aid in laying out parcels of land, in construction, and for storage. Little, if any, evidence from the 2nd or 3rd millennia BCE reveals progress in mathematical abstractions.

[104] The Pythagorean school relied heavily on Egyptian concepts, including numbers which, it turns out, were an impediment to be overcome later by Indian and Mesopotamian numbers.

[105] Herbert Turnbull writes in *The Great Mathematicians:* "A distinctive badge of the brotherhood was the beautiful star pentagon a fit symbol of the mathematics which the school discovered. It was also the symbol of health. Indeed, the Pythagoreans were specially interested in the study of medicine" (Newman, 1956, p. 83).

[106] Testament to the clarity of Euclid's *Elements* and his other works is a whole body of study known as "non-Euclidean" geometry. Good argument, mathematical or otherwise, enables clarity of understanding, constructive analysis, and critique.

[107] For a compact, fairly recent overview of the philosophy of science, see Okasha (2002). Curd and Cover (1998) provide a more extensive treatment.

[108] Copernicus had developed an early version of his heliocentric theory of the universe in 1512, just before Luther nailed his 95 theses to the door of Wittenberg castle. It was a time of religious and intellectual ferment, and a time of ruthless reaction by the Church to arguments deemed threatening. But Durant offers an interesting contention about the progress of science in the early 15th century: "The superstitions of the people, rather than the opposition of the Church retarded the development

of science... until the Counter Reformation that followed the Council of Trent (1545)" (Durant, 1953, pt V, pp. 528-9).

[109] Russell, for example, describes the extensive astronomical works of Aristarchus of Samos, around 200 BCE, that included a heliocentric model of the universe and some remarkably accurate estimates of the spherical earth and distances between planets (Russell, 1945, pp. 214-6).

[110] Interesting that Charles Peirce, founder of pragmatism, coined the word "tychism" (*tyche* is Greek for chance) to assert or indicate chance in the universe, as against determinism. Contrast this with Einstein's comment that "God does not play dice with the universe." How shall we have it?

[111] Newton's law, roughly stated, is that objects attract one another proportionately to the product of their masses and inversely to the square between them.

[112] The first logical positivists included Rudolph Carnap, Herbert Feigl, A.J. Ayer, and Ernest Nagel, some of whom migrated from Europe in the early 20th century. One of their notable projects was the *Encyclopedia of Unified Science*, a collection of articles on science methodology.

[113] As part of a long argument against the logical positive perception of science, Popper argues against their induction content and devotes his volume, *The Logic of Scientific Discovery,* to the idea of falsifiability. In his words: "...I shall not require of a scientific system that it shall be capable of being singled out, once and for all, in a positive sense; but I shall require that its logical form shall be such that it can be singled out, by means of empirical tests, in a negative sense: it must be possible for an empirical scientific system to be refuted by experience" (Popper, 1961, p. 41).

[114] In a 1969 postscript, Kuhn offered "disciplinary matrix" as an alternative to the term "paradigm" (Kuhn, 1996, p. 182).

[115] As preparation to support his paradigm shift approach, Kuhn criticizes the positivistic approach, including Popper, by arguing: "Popper's anomalous experience is important to science because it evokes competitors for an existing paradigm. But falsification, though it surely occurs, does not happen with, or simply because of the emergence of an anomaly or falsifying instance" (Kuhn, 1996, p. 170).

[116] Durant, 1954. *Our Oriental Heritage,* p. 104. The Durants' encyclopedic history of civilization was completed in 10 volumes, published separately between 1939 and 1967, the first 6 of which are shown authored by Will Durant and last 4 by Will and Ariel Durant. General attribution is shown as Durant, 1939-67, and quotes with volume, publication year, and page numbers.

To complicate the chronology, Durant(s) arrange the narration in five parts, wherein the publication date of Part I, "Our Oriental Heritage," in 1954 treats the earliest historical period rather than Parts II, and III, which were published in 1939 and 1950. Nevertheless, their "Story of Civilization" is a treasury of historical writing.

[117] An interesting aside to the year 1400 BCE is that it is a traditional approximation of the death of Moses. By that time a phonetic alphabet existed, but probably not available to Moses on Mt. Sinai. The Ten Commandments must have been inscribed in cuneiform on the tablets of stone (e.g., Exodus 24:12). "Stone" tablet was clay?

[118] The fascinating story of cuneiform decipherment is told in Andrew Robinson's *The Story of Writing* (Robinson, 1995, pp. 71-91). About 1,500 years after the last cuneiform inscriptions were formed, they were discovered by European scholars, and not until the 1770s was decipherment started by a Danish traveler Carsten Niebuhr and continued by Grotefend, Rawlinson, and others into the late 19th century.

[119] Soon thereafter, Thomas Jefferson sold his entire collection of 6,487 books to Congress, more than doubling the number before the burning by the British.

[120] No better illustration is man/dog communication. Stanley Coren, in *How to Speak Dog* (NY: Free Press, 2000), emphasizes the distinction and relation between understanding and producing language. He creates a dictionary of over 50 human words commonly heard and understood by dogs, but which, of course, they cannot produce. It would be a rare human that understood that many dog "words."

[121] The number of languages varies widely depending on the definition and classification of language. Suffice here to say the number is very large, but dominated by very few—say, less than a dozen—as measured by number of speakers. Mandarin, English, and Spanish are the three most common languages, with English perhaps the closest to an international language. That half the languages will die within the 21st century is based on Claude Hagege's *On the Death and Life of Languages, 2009.* That estimation is based on 5,000 languages, dying at the rate of 25 per year.

[122] Carlos Carrion Torres, in "English as a Universal Language," (*Omniglot,* 04 Dec. 2009, p. 1), writes: "English is without a doubt the actual universal language. It is the world's second largest native language, the official language in 70 countries, and English-speaking countries are responsible for about 40% of world's total GNP...English can be at least understood almost everywhere among scholars and educated people, as it is the world media language... [It] is one of the simplest and easiest natural languages in the world..." This short online article summarizes the reasons why English is useful as a language.

[123] The impact on reading and thinking is of some concern among those analyzing the form and uses of electronic media. Rebecca Rosen, in the *Wilson Quarterly*, concludes that "...the

most salient difference isn't between a screen and a page but between focused reading and disjointed scanning... Marshall Poe observes, 'A book is a machine for focusing attention, the Internet is machine for diffusing it.'" Clearly, writing aided the development of reasoning and preservation of facts, ingredients of detection, reflection, and correction.

[124] In the latter half of the 20th century, we witnessed another major cultural shift caused by the medium, largely instant global mobile electronic technology. Marshall McLuhan aptly phrased it "the medium is the message." One feature is extension of pictographic forms. It is easier to lie with a picture than words, or perhaps more precisely, to encourage indifference to what Goody (1986) called "the logic of writing." The emergence of electronic babble, with a mosaic of pictures and unstructured word collections directed to emotive or entertainment ends, could overwhelm the strength of writing—detection for correction.

[125] The write-up of the Commandments delivery story in Exodus 20:1-17 and the rest of the Exodus story is the subject of much biblical scholarship and controversy. Without entering an argument about either authorship or its dates, the question about writing remains. Indeed, the validity of commandment principles would seem fairly authoritative on their content, regardless of an inscription on stone.

[126] The final words of Hawking's *A Brief History of Time* (Hawking, 1988).

[127] Karen Armstrong, in her opening of *The History of God*, notes: "In Babylonian myth—as later in the Bible—there was no creation out of nothing, an idea that was alien to the ancient world. Before either the gods or human beings existed, this sacred raw material had existed from all eternity... In the *Enuma Elish*, chaos is not a fiery, seething mass... but a sloppy mess where everything lacks boundary, definition and identity" (p.7).

[128] By most accountings, there are at least 26, many with overlapping functions, rivalries, and struggles.

[129] Olaf Skotkonung, king of Sweden, was baptized about 1000 CE. This was the time Sweden was forming as a nation, and a time when Scandinavians were making landfall on North America. By 1520, political struggles within the Kalmar union, combined with enforcement of church orthodoxy, resulted in the Stockholm blood bath. Many Swedish nobles were executed for heresy. Bloodshed to enforce "beliefs" is not uncommon in the history of civilization.

[130] The creation myths are told in thumbnail fashion by Hamilton and attractively illustrated by Barry Moser (Hamilton, 1988).

[131] Heaven and or the universe may have been accounted for by the "dome of light" (Gen 1:14-17) surrounding earth. Creation may have been a seven-day project if a seventh day for rest is included.

[132] In the New Oxford Annotated Bible, God is referenced in the plural (Gen 1:26), whereas prior declarations are shown singular. There is no account of God in plural prior to that.

[133] Dekkers wrote: "In past centuries, commoners' sitting rooms often had a "Stairway of Life" hanging on their walls...drawn, printed, embroidered, or carved..." (Dekkers, 1997, p.4). He emphasized that the stairway peaked not at the end of life but somewhere in midlife, thus indicating a period of decline before termination and suggesting the subtitle to his book "The Romance of Ruins." As I have indicated elsewhere, he was describing not a stairway but a stile (and so inviting the pun-ish "life stile").

[134] By some accounts, only humans are conscious of death, but other species, aware or not, do seem to make efforts to defer it with every instinct and means available. Because we cannot access the body of myths, if any, held by other species, we are limited to our own. And even within our own species, there

do appear to be differences in the perspective of death and its consequences.

[135] A cultural inheritance of the time when the Bible was written, the snake symbolized knowledge. Note, for example, that a serpent figures prominently in many symbols for medicine and healing.

[136] The number of commandments in each element varies by version, but a common division is 4 God/authority and 6 behavior directives, with differing clustering of instructions (Exodus 2:2-17 and 34:11-27; Deuteronomy 5: 6-21).

[137] Worded in the New Oxford Annotated Bible as: "Then God said, 'Let us make humankind in our image, according to our likeness...'" With the plural interpreted in this Bible version as "divine beings who compose God's heavenly court."

[138] Falvey considers sustainability as "a proxy for immortality or rebirth" and that it reveals "a fundamental fear of impermanence" (Falvey, 2005, p. 260).

[139] The Greek version of Zarathustra is the commonly used Zoroaster.

[140] See, for example, Rivetna (2009) or Boyce (1984).

[141] For this reason, those unfamiliar with Zarathustrism thought of it as "fire worship." It is, of course, no more fire worship than Christianity is cross worship.

[142] Hippocrates (460-370 BCE—contemporary of Socrates). Many versions of the Hippocratic Oath are available. These are the opening words of what is labeled "classical version" and translated from the Greek by Ludwig Edelstein, and displayed in www.medterms.com. There is some question about the original authorship, including the possibility of composition by the Pythagoreans. In any case, it has so evolved that a modern physician would recite a version differing markedly from the original.

[143] Progress in medicine continues under the mantle of science, leaving less of diagnosis and healing to miraculous forces of

nature by whatever name. That progress further separates the domains of religion and medicine to their respective strengths. Recently, an international doctors' panel appointed by the Roman Catholic Church says it is getting out of the 'miracle' business at Lourdes. The panel said that from now on it will rule only on whether healing cases at the French shrine are 'remarkable,' leaving it to the church to decide whether they are miracles" (*Washington Post*, December 4, 2008, p. A14).

[144] Gould argues the NOMA principle, i.e., No Overlapping Magisteria: "...the net or magisterium of science covers the empirical realm...The magisterium of religion extends over questions of ultimate meaning and moral value. These two magisteria do not overlap..." (Gould, 1999, p. 6).

[145] Greider, 1987, p. 234. Further, Greider writes: "Money, like religion, unified life's contradictions—the petty and the exalted, the confusing multiplicity of things and the elemental, immutable truths, the limits and the potential described by life and death."

[146] One version in the Bible (Exodus 20: 2-17) has God speaking directly to the Israelites. In another version (Exodus 34: 11-27), the message is on tablets of stone. Exodus 32:16 has the covenant in writing on stone: "The tablets were the work of God, and the writing was the writing of God, engraved upon the tablets" (Exodus 32:16).

[147] The definitional question raised may stray from the purported intent of the book to present Jesus as the "incarnate Word of God" and fleshly aspect of the divine (Bible, New Testament, p.146 *passim*). Karen Armstrong explains that through Paul, "Christians would come to see Jesus as an avatar of God...to save the human race...." (Armstrong, 2006, p. 383). Perhaps my perspective is more literary than theological, but useful discourse seems to call for definitions, especially of God.

[148] Atheists and believers argue about the existence of God, seldom if ever defining Him/Her/It/They.

<sup>149</sup> Friedman, in Hausman, 1984, pp. 369, 223.

<sup>150</sup> Vaihinger, 1968. His "as if" concept essentially sidesteps notions of truth in the usual sense of the word (versus validity in Aristotelian logic) and treats a theory as a convenient fiction.

<sup>151</sup> Ogden, 1932. The latter half of Ogden's book contains a mosaic of Bentham's extant theory of fictions writings. Jeremy Bentham's (1748-1832) complete works are in multiple volumes, assembled by his nephew John Bowring. References to Bentham here draw generally from Ogden's book.

<sup>152</sup> J.H. Burton on Bentham's fictions of law (Ogden, 1932, p. xvii).

<sup>153</sup> Bentham was one of the founders of the utilitarian philosophy. His perspective, therefore, is consequentialist and perhaps thus, in modern-day terms, compatible with many religious approaches to morals or ethics. The consequentialist perspective of ethics is essentially that one should do X, *because it will lead to*, say, happiness, salvation, redemption, etc. By contrast, the deontological perspective states ethical rules to be upheld regardless of consequences—that is, do right because it is right.

<sup>154</sup> Vaihinger, 1968, p. xxiv.

<sup>155</sup> Vaihinger 1968, pp. 184-8. According to Ogden, Vaihinger became aware of Bentham's work late in his studies, by which time he was seriously vision-impaired. Thus dependence on, and reference to, Bentham was minimal.

<sup>156</sup> Vaihinger, 1968, p. 316.

<sup>157</sup> Vaihinger, 1968, p. 328.

<sup>158</sup> In his *Shakespeare's God,* Ivor Morris uses the tragedies of Macbeth, Othello, King Lear, and Hamlet to relate religion to the content of Shakespeare's plays. While containing some recognizable insights, his opaque dissertation mentions religion a lot, but doesn't address the nature of God. The reader might absorb the moral lesson of King Lear more enjoyably by reading Jane Smiley's *A Thousand Acres*.

[159] Wright, 1936, p. 1020.

[160] In his *Life of Greece,* Durant writes: "About 300 Euhemerus of Messina in Sicily published his *Hiera Anagrapha* (literally *Holy Scriptures,* or *Records*), in which he argued that the gods were either personified powers of nature, or, more often, human heroes deified by popular imagination or gratitude for their benefits to mankind; that myths were allegories, and that religious ceremonies were originally exercises in commemoration of the dead...." (Durant, 1939, p. 565).

# Readings

Ackrill, J.L. (ed). 1987. *A New Aristotle Reader*, NJ: Princeton University Press.

Adams, Henry. 1931. *The Education of Henry Adams {1918}*, NY: The Modern Library.

Akerlof, George, and R. Shiller. 2009. *Animal Spirits*, Princeton: Princeton University Press.

Anonymous. 2007. "Ears of Plenty: The story of man's staple food," www.The Economist.com (from *The Economist*, December 20, 2005 print edition).

Armstrong, Karen. 1993. *A History of God: The 4,000 Year Quest of Judaism, Christianity and Islam*, NY: Ballantine Books.

Armstrong, Karen. 2006. *The Great Transformation: The Beginnings of Our Religious Traditions*, NY: Alfred A. Knopf.

Aristotle. 2007. *On the Motion of Animals*, translation by A. Farquharson, www.ebooks.adelaide.edu.

Ashworth, William. 2006. *Ogallala Blue: Water and Life on the High Plains*, Woodstock, VT: The Countryman Press.

Bartlett, Albert. 2004. *The Essential Exponential: For the Future of Our Planet*, Lincoln, NE: Center for Science, Mathematics and Computer Education.

Bartlett, Frederick. 1958. *Thinking: An Experimental and Social Study {1958}*, Westport, CT: Greenwood Press.

Berry, Wendell. 1985. *Collected Poems*, San Francisco: North Point Press.

Boulding, Kenneth. 1962. *Conflict and Defense: A General Theory*, NY: Harper and Row.

Boyce, Mary (ed.). 1984. *Textual Sources for the Study of Zoroastrianism*, Manchester: Manchester University Press.

Bronowski, Jacob. 1973. *The Ascent of Man*, Boston: Little, Brown and Company.

Buck, B.A. 1982. "Ancient Technology in Contemporary Surgery," *Western Journal of Medicine*, 136, pp. 265-9.

Buckland, Richard 1983. "Comparative structure and evolution of goat and sheep satellite I DNAs," *Nucleic Acids Research*, vol. 11, No. 5, pp. 1349-59.

Callicott, Baird, and R. Frodeman, (eds). 2009. *Encyclopedia of Environmental Ethics and Philosophy*, Detroit: Gale Cengage Learning, Macmillan Reference USA.

Cantillon, Richard.1964. *Essai sur la Nature du Commerce en Generale {1755},* NY: Augustus Kelley.

Cauvin, Jacques. 2000 [French edition, 1994]. *The Birth of the Gods and the Origins of Agriculture* [translated: Trevor Watkins], Cambridge: Cambridge University Press.

Coogan, Michael et al. (eds.). 2001. *The New Oxford Annotated Bible,* NY: Oxford University Press.

Copi, Irving. 1986. *Introduction to Logic,* NY: Macmillan.

Cohen, Morris, and E. Nagel. 1962. *Introduction to Logic,* NY: Harcourt, Brace.

Connolly, William. 2008. *Capitalism and Christianity, American Style,* Durham: Duke University Press.

Cramb, Alan. 2008. A Short History of Metals, www.neon.mems.cmu.edu

Curd, Martin, and J. Cover. 1998. *Philosophy of Science: The Central Issues,* NY: Norton.

Darston, Robert. 2010. "Can We Create a National Digital Library?" *The New York Review of Books,* Oct. 28, 2010, p. 4.

Dary, David. 1974. *The Buffalo Book,* Chicago: Sage Books.

Dekkers, Midas. 1997. *The Way of All Flesh: The Romance of Ruins,* NY: Farrar, Straus, and Giroux.

Diamond, Jared. 1997. *Guns, Germs, and Steel*, NY: W.W. Norton.

Dougherty, Jude P. 2003. *The Logic of Religion*, Washington, DC: The Catholic University Press.

Dovring, Folke. 1987. *Land Economics*, Boston: Breton Publishers.

Dovring, Folke. 1998. *Knowledge and Ignorance: Essays on Lights and Shadows*, Westport, CT: Praeger.

Durant, Will, and A. Durant. 1939-1967. *The Story of Civilization*, NY: Simon and Schuster.

Durant, Will. 1953. *The Story of Philosophy*, NY: Simon and Schuster.

Eatwell, John, M. Milgate, and P. Newman. 1987. *The New Palgrave: A Dictionary of Economics,* NY: Macmillan Press.

Energy Information Administration (EIA). 2010. Table 1.1 Net Generation [electricity] by Energy Source, *Electric Power Monthly*. www.eia.doe.gov.

Falvey, Lindsay. 2005. *Religion and Agriculture: Sustainability in Christianity and Buddhism*, online for Adelaide: Institute for International Development.

Federico, Giovanni. 2005. *Feeding the World: An Economic History of Agriculture, 1800-2000*, Princeton, NJ: Princeton University Press.

Ferguson, Niall. 2008. *The Ascent of Money: A Financial History of the World*, NY: The Penguin Press.

Fischer, Steven. 2001. *A History of Writing*, London: Reaction Books.

Frankfurt, Harry. 2005. *On Bullshit*, Princeton, NJ: Princeton University Press.

Frankfurt, Harry. 2006. *On Truth*. NY: Alfred Knopf.

Friedman, M., and G. Friedland. 1998. *Medicine's 10 Greatest Discoveries*, New Haven, CT: Yale University Press.

Galbraith, J. Kenneth. 1975. *Money: Whence It Came Where It Went*, Boston: Houghton Mifflin.

Goody, Jack. 1988. *The Logic of Writing and the Organization of Society*, Cambridge: Cambridge University Press.

Gould, Stephen Jay. 1999. *Rocks of Ages*, NY: Ballantine Books.

Greider, William. 1987. *Secrets of the Temple: How the Federal Reserve Runs the Country*, NY: Simon and Schuster.

Greider, William. 2009. "Fixing the Fed," *The Nation*, vol. 288, no.12, pp. 18-22.

Hamilton, Virginia. 1988. *In the Beginning: Creation Stories from Around the World*, NY: Harcourt Brace.

Harlan, Jack R. 1995. *The Living Fields: Our Agricultural Heritage*, Cambridge: Cambridge University Press.

Hausman, Daniel. 1984. *The Philosophy of Economics*, Cambridge: Cambridge University Press.

Hawking, Stephen (ed.). 2005. *God Created the Integers: The Mathematical Breakthroughs That Changed History*, Philadelphia: Running Press.

Heiser, Charles B. 1990. *Seed to Civilization: The Story of Food*, Cambridge, MA: Harvard University Press.

Helms, Douglas, and D. Bowers (eds.). 1994. *The History of Agriculture and the Environment*, Washington, DC: The Agricultural History Society.

Hesser, Leon. 2006. *The Man Who Fed the World*, Dallas: Durban House Publishing.

Hippocrates. 1952. "Hippocratic Writings" in Robert Maynard Hutchins (ed.), *Great Books of the Western World*, Chicago: Encyclopedia Britannica.

Hitchcock, A.S. {1935} Revised, Agnes Chase.1950. *Manual of the Grasses*, U.S. Dept. of Agriculture, Misc. Pub. 200, Washington, DC: Government Printing Office.

Hobbes, Thomas. 1950. *Leviathan {1651}*, NY: E.P. Dutton

Hobhouse, Henry. 1985. *Seeds of Change: Five Plants That Transformed Mankind,* NY: Harper and Row.

Honderich, Ted. 1995. *The Oxford Companion to Philosophy*, Oxford: Oxford University Press.

Hoppe, Robert, and D. Banker. 2010. *Structure and Finances of U.S. Farms: Family Farm Report, 2010 Edition,* EIB-66, Washington, DC : U.S. Dept. of Agriculture..

International Energy Agency. 2008. *Key World Energy Statistics*, Paris.

Jutte, Robert. 2008. *Contraception: A History {2003}*, Cambridge: Polity Press.

Keynes, J.M. 1958. *A Treatise on Money {1930}*, London: Macmillan and Co.

Keynes, J.M. 1961. *The General Theory of Employment, Interest, and Money {1936}*, NY: Macmillan and Co.

Kirk, G.S., J. Raven, and M. Schofield. 1983. *The Pre-Socratic Philosophers*, Cambridge: Cambridge University Press.

Kneale, William, and M. Kneale. 1986. *The Development of Logic*, Oxford: Clarendon Press.

Kuchler, Fred, and E. Golan. 1999. *Assigning Values to Life: Comparing Methods for Valuing Health Risks*, U.S. Department of Agriculture, AER-784, Washington, DC.

Kuhn, Thomas. 1996. *The Structure of Scientific Revolutions {1962}*, Chicago: University of Chicago Press.

Kuijt, Ian, and B. Finlayson. 2009. "Evidence for Food Storage and Predomestication Granaries 11,000 Years Ago in the Jordan Valley," in *Proceedings of the National Academy of Science*, July 7, 2009, pp. 10966-10970.

Lake, Larry, R. Schmidt, and P. Veneto. 1992. "A Niche for Enhanced Oil Recovery in the 1990s," *Oilfield Review*.

Leakey, Richard and R Lewin. 1992. *Origins Reconsidered: In Search of What Makes Us Human,* NY: Doubleday.

Lockwood, Charles. 2007. *The Human Story: Where We Come From and How We Evolved,* London: Natural History Museum.

Massachusetts Institute of Technology. 2006. *The Future of Geothermal Energy: Impact of Enhanced Geothermal Systems on the United States in the 21ˢᵗ Century,* U.S. Department of Energy: Idaho National Laboratory

McKibben, Bill. 1989. *The End of Nature,* NY: Random House.

Merwin, W.S. 2005. *Migration: New and Selected Poems,* Port Townsend, WA: Copper Canyon Press.

Metzer, Bruce, and M. Coogan (eds.). 1993. *The Oxford Companion to the Bible,* NY: Oxford University Press.

Miller, Naomi, and K. Gleason. 1994. "Fertilizer in the Identification and Analysis of Cultivated Soil," *The Archaeology of Garden and Field,* Philadelphia: Univ. of Pennsylvania Press.

Morris, Ivor. 1972. *Shakespeare's God: The Role of Religion in the Tragedies,* London: George Allen and Unwin Ltd.

Mumford, Lewis. 1961. *The City in History: Its Origins, Its Transformations, and Its Prospects,* NY: Harcourt Brace and World, Inc.

National Research Council. 2000. *Beyond Six Billion: Forecasting the World's Population,* Washington, DC: National Academy Press.

Nelson, Robert. 2009. *The New Holy Wars: Economic Religion Versus Environmental Religion in Contemporary America*, State College, PA: Penn State University Press.

Nesbitt, Mark. 2001. "Wheat evolution: integrating archaeological and biological evidence," in P.D.S. Caligari and P, Brandham (eds.), *Wheat taxonomy: the legacy of John Percival*, pp. 37-59, London: Linnean Society, Special Issue 3.

Newman, James. 1956. *The World of Mathematics*, NY: Simon and Schuster.

Nietzsche, Frederick. 1980. *On the Advantages and Disadvantage of History for Life {1874}*, Indianapolis: Hackett Publishing.

Oates, J.C.T. 1975. *Cambridge University Library: A Historical Sketch*, Cambridge: Cambridge University Library. www.lib.cam.ac.uk/history.

Ogden, Charles K. 1932. *Bentham's Theory of Fictions*, London: Kegan Paul, Trench, Trubner.

Okasha, Samir. 2002. *Philosophy of Science: A Very Short Introduction*, NY: Oxford University Press.

Pei, Mario. 1965. *The Story of Language*, NY: J.B. Lippincott Company.

Pollan, Michael. 2007. *Omnivore's Dilemma: A Natural History of Four Meals*, NY: Penguin Books.

Popper, Karl. 1961. *The Logic of Scientific Discovery*, NY: Science Editions.

Porter, Roy (ed.). 1997. *Medicine: A History of Healing*, NY: Marlowe & Company.

Porter, Roy. 1997. *The Greatest Benefit to Mankind*, NY: Norton & Company.

Psillos, Stathis, and M. Curd (eds.). 2008. *The Routledge Companion to Philosophy of Science*, NY: Routledge.

Rahimi, Scott, D. McDonnell, A. Ahmadi, and J. Vende. 2007. "Medieval neurosurgery: contributions from the Middle East, Spain, and Persia," *Neurosurgical Focus*, vol. 23, July, pp. 1-4.

Rasmussen, Wayne (ed.) 1960. *Readings in the History of American Agriculture*, Urbana: University of Illinois Press.

Reed, Charles A. (ed.). 1977. *Origins of Agriculture*, The Hague: Mouton Publishers.

Rindos, David. 1984. *The Origins of Agriculture: An Evolutionary Perspective*, Orlando, FL: Academic Press.

Rivetna, Roshan (ed.). 2002. *The Legacy of Zarathustra*, Hinsdale, IL: Fezana.

Robinson, Andrew. 1995. *The Story of Writing*, London: Thames and Hudson.

Rosen, Rebecca. 2009. "In the Beginning Was the Word," *The Wilson Quarterly*, vol. 33, no. 4, August.

Russell, Bertrand. 1945. *A History of Western Philosophy*, NY: Simon and Schuster.

Samaras, Thomas (ed.). 2007. *Human Body Size and the Laws of Scaling: Physiological, Performance, Growth, Longevity and Ecological Ramifications*, NY: Nova Science Publishers.

Schumpeter, Joseph. 1976. *Capitalism, Socialism, and Democracy {1942},* NY: Harper and Row.

Schleidt, Wolfgang and M. Shalter. 2003. "Co-evolution of Humans and Canids: An Alternative View of Dog Domestication," *Evolution and Cognition*, vol. 9, no. 1, pp. 57-72.

Schumacher, E.F. 1973. *Small is Beautiful: Economics as if People Mattered*, NY: Harper Torchbooks.

Seife, Charles. 2000. *Zero: The Biography of a Dangerous Idea*, NY: Penguin

Shiller, Robert. 1998. *Indexed Units of Account: Theory and Assessment of Historical Experience*, Report #1171. New Haven, CT: Cowles Commission.

Smiley, Jane. 1991. *A Thousand Acres*, NY: Alfred Knopf.

Smith, Adam. 1937. *The Wealth of Nations {1776},* NY: The Modern Library.

Stallknecht, G.F, K. Gilbertson, and J. Ranney. 1996. "Alternative wheat cereals as food grains: Einkorn, emmer, spelt, kamut, and triticale," in J. Janick (ed.), *Progress in New Crops*. pp. 156-170, Alexandria, VA: ASHS Press.

Tester, Jefferson, Elisabeth M. Drake, Michael J. Driscoll, Michael W. Golay, and William A. Peters. 2005. *Sustainable Energy: Choosing Among Options.* Cambridge, MA: The MIT Press.

Thompson, Paul. 1995. *The Spirit of the Soil: Agriculture and Environmental Ethics*, NY: Routledge.

Toynbee, Arnold. 1976. *Mankind and Mother Earth: A Narrative History of the World*, NY: Oxford University Press.

U.S. Census Bureau. 2008. Historical Estimates of World Population, www.census.gov.

U.S. Department of Agriculture. 1963. *A Century of Service: The First 100 years of the United States Department of Agriculture*, Washington, DC.

U.S. Department of Energy. 2010. *U.S. Primary Energy Flow by Source and Sector, 2009*. Annual Energy Review, August 2010, www. eia.doe.gov/aer/pccss.

U.S. Department of Energy. 2010. *World Energy Demand and Outlook, 2010,* International Energy Outlook.www.eia.doe.gov/ oiaf/ieo/world.

Vasey, Daniel. 1992. *An Ecological History of Agriculture: 10,000 B.C.- A.D 10,000*, Ames, IA: Iowa State University Press.

Vaihinger, Hans. 1968. *The Philosophy of 'As If:' A System of the Theoretical, Practical and Religious Fictions of Mankind {1924},* NY: Barnes and Noble.

Vidal, Gore. 1981. *Creation*, NY: Random Books.

Watson, Peter. 2006. *Ideas: A History of Thought and Invention, from Fire to Freud*, NY: Harper Perennial.

Wilson, Edward O. 2006. *The Creation: An Appeal to Save Life on Earth,* NY: W.W. Norton & Company.

White, Leslie. 1956. "The Locus of Mathematical Reality: An Anthropological Footnote," in J. Newman (ed.), *The World of Mathematics*, NY: Simon and Schuster.

Whitehead, Alfred. 1956. "Mathematics as an Element in the History of Thought," in James Newman (ed.), *The World of Mathematics*, pp. 402-419, NY: Simon and Schuster.

Wright, William (ed). 1936. *The Complete Works of William Shakespeare,* NY: Garden City Books.

Young, J.Z. 1971. *Introduction to the Study of Man*, NY: Oxford University Press.

Zuckerman, Larry. 1998. *The Potato: How the Humble Spud Rescued the Western World*, Boston: Faber and Faber.